All is Well Within My Soul

Finding Peace and Purpose in the Aftermath of Abuse

All is Well Within My Soul

Finding Peace and Purpose in the Aftermath of Abuse

VICKI HAIDEK

with Tamara Pray Frazier

ISBN: 978-1-7361667-1-0 (hardcover)

978-1-7361667-0-3 (paperback)

978-1-7361667-2-7 (ebook

Cover Art by: Tunisa Rice

Copies may be ordered from:

www.myjourneysda.org

MANUFACTURED IN THE UNITED STATES OF AMERica

Dedication

For Araceli...

While you are no longer here in the physical, I still feel your presence every day, guiding, and encouraging me to believe in myself and take control of my destiny. You believed in me and invested in me; you never asked for anything in return except for me to Journey On and make a difference in the lives of other victims of domestic violence. I will never stop working to make sure our mission at My Journey Stop Domestic Abuse is fulfilled and your kindness is paid forward. I love and miss you every day...

Vicki

Acknowledgements

THANK YOU first and foremost to my Lord and Savior Jesus Christ. You have done a mighty work in me! Thank you for loving me through all of my faults and frailties and for forgiving me over and over again as I struggled to find my way. You are my light in the darkness and I would be nothing without you.

Shonda Mickel, I sincerely thank you for allowing God to use you 27 years ago when I was released from prison. If you had not believed in me and trusted the God in me I don't know where I would be. You took a chance on a convicted felon and taught me everything I needed to know in preparation for me to one day work for myself. It is because of you that I now run a successful Income Tax Business and that gift of entrepreneurship has been the cornerstone to every subsequent business I have birthed. You have always been more than a boss; you are a trusted confidant, sister and friend and I sincerely thank you for the laughter, lessons and most of all, Love.

Tamara, I know I tell you this all the time, but I want the world to know that I love you and appreciate you for everything; from birthing this book to keeping me grounded and focused. I thank God for allowing our paths to cross yet again.

As iron sharpens iron, one man sharpens another

~Proverbs 27:17

Table of Contents

Foreword

The warden said, "Young lady, what is wrong with you?"

Asking that question to a wounded child no matter their chronological age who has endured physical, emotional, or sexual trauma only inflicts more trauma on the individual. Immediately, judgement is imposed on the individual.

According to the National Child Traumatic Stress Initiative 2 out of 3 children reported at least one traumatic event by age 16. Other people, like the author, have possibly experienced more than one traumatic event by age 16.

Childhood trauma significantly impacts a child's emotional health and neurological development.

Research has proven that complex trauma changes or alters the brain of the affected child.

Focus for Health completed studies that reported grave statistics.

- Incarcerated women were almost twice as likely to report a history of childhood sexual or physical abuse compared to those not incarcerated.

- Almost half (5 out of 10) of those pregnant as teenagers have a history of childhood sexual abuse.

- A study of individuals in an inpatient alcohol detoxification unit found 81% of women and 69% of men disclosed a history of sexual and or physical abuse.

- People who experience violence as children, including physical and sexual abuse, are more likely to drop out of high school (Girls by 24% Boys by 26%).

The vulnerability and courage that Vicki Haidek expresses while sharing her story is paramount considering her troubled upbringing. Although her life from childhood through a portion of adulthood has been characterized as turbulent, there has remained one constant or anchor during those tempestuous times – her unrelenting faith in God.

For those reasons, I am both humbled and honored to pen this foreword. My sister in Christ, Vicki Haidek, is a supreme survivor of childhood atrocities who unintentionally welcomed all stages of domestic violence into her world. Her words are heartfelt, painful, yet sincere; therefore, I am proud to introduce an eloquently crafted piece that will challenge us to prioritize our thoughts. Let us always seek to understand first, rather than to judge.

The warden said, "Young lady, what happened to you?"

Tamara Bogan,
Licensed Psychotherapist

Pardon Me, Please

Good Afternoon.
My name is Vicki Golden and I am a Survivor of Domestic Abuse. I am writing to you because I seek a solution to some very debilitating issues I have been battling for the last 25 plus years. I've tried to deal with them on my own; through counseling and advocating for other victims of abuse. I've prayed and sought help through the court system, to no avail. It is my prayer that I can reach someone of influence who has contacts from all walks of life; in the hopes that they may know someone who knows someone who can help me. The strong woman of God that I am today is a living, breathing testament that no matter what set of circumstances life hands you, if you have the will, there is a way out. Today I am living an amazingly beautiful and full life despite having lived through a 17-year cycle

of physical, mental and emotional abuse that started at a very young age. I am living, loving, and learning to laugh in the face of adversity because the **Violence** in my life was not victorious! Those **Problems** did not prevail! My **Trials** did not triumph and all the **Battering** and **Bruises** did not break me! I am living my life in spite of everything that I went through and continue to go through in the aftermath of domestic abuse; yet one issue drags on doggedly.

I have lived the nightmare of domestic abuse and through God's grace and mercy I survived! Not only did I survive but I have been able to recover a large portion of my life or should I say I have been able to begin living a real life, for my life prior to the violence was marred with tragedy and abuse as well. My story is one of triumph over adversity when so many of life's cards were stacked against me and continued to build up until I had a huge mountain of despair staring me in the face at the age of 21. I was a young wife and mother of three and I was placed under arrest as I stood in front of police officers covered in my husband's blood — charged with aggravated assault. But to understand how I arrived at that heartbreaking place at such a tender, young age, I will have to take you back to my childhood and visit my upbringing; losing my mother to *prison at an early age, rape, teenage pregnancy and marriage to my abuser at 16; a man almost twice my age... Prison. I have overcome so much adversity in the twenty years since my release. No, it hasn't been a bed of roses but I'm still standing! I've made many strides, yet there are still many rivers to cross; namely the doors that constantly close in my face because I am a convicted felon. There are so many things I have yet to experience in this lifetime and would love the opportunity to try. While I love being an entrepreneur I would love the option of going through the entire job interview process, but I have yet to get past the application phase. I know for many this is a small thing but I guess it's the "little things" that everyone else takes for granted that escape me. I've consulted with many agencies, and sought the advice of many experts, but none thus far has been able to tell me how I can fix the important things that are still broken in my life. With God's help I've managed to repair many of the broken relationships that were lost. He's allowed me to forgive myself for so many things; namely, undervaluing myself and staying in broken relationships. I only pray there is an answer to how I can break down the barriers that bar me from the simple comfort of hearing the words "Background Check" and not break into a cold sweat...I cannot explain the pain and hurt my heart feels when I see the look of alarm, mixed with disdain in someone's eyes after they've checked my background. I've come to recognize it over the years, for it is the one thing that has the ability to remind me of the painful past I suffered because of domestic abuse.*

I am not a complicated person and my needs are few. I am resilient, courageous and truly satisfied with the many blessings God has afforded me, as I know my life could be so much worse coming from where I've been!! That is why I am soliciting advice, assistance and direction for my issue because I really feel like there is someone out there who can help me! It took a long time before I was strong enough to begin my journey back to me, but what's important is that I took that first step. It's been a huge uphill climb and thankfully I had a couple of guardian angels in my path because I could not have done it alone! They pushed me, pulled me, held me up and got me to the top of that Mountain of despair! Healing is a never-ending walk but now that I have arrived at that safe, happy, healing place, I am now ready to build upon my foundation...Once again, I am seeking God to dispatch his guardian angels – only this time I require less pushing, and pulling to achieve my goal.

I Am Ready! At this time, prayerfully, guidance, under-standing and compassion is all I stand in the need of... Pardon Me, Please.

Sincerely,
Vicky Golden

Excerpts from the letter to the State of Georgia Board of Pardons and Paroles.

Book One

The Honeymoon Phase...

Self-Preservation...That is the term that immediately comes to mind when I think about how I made it through some of the more traumatic experiences in my life. Truthfully, I don't necessarily like using that word because in some instances preserving one's self means you have to sacrifice others and that is definitely not a good thing when you are a wife and mother. And too, I believe there is a fine line between self-preservation and just being plain old selfish that we can unintentionally cross if we are not careful in our pursuit of survival. My life story is mixed with both; marred by tragedy, dysfunction, and abuse, but alas, I am still here—and for that I am extremely thankful.

Living on the edge of chaos brought on by abuse and dysfunction has a way of compromising our ability to build and maintain solid relationships no matter how much we would love to love and be loved properly...So no, I don't like talking about self-preservation, but if I am going to tell my story, then I am going to tell the truth, whether I like it or not. My story is one of triumph after much adversity! In my first 25 years of life, I experienced more trauma and trepidation than some people will experience in a lifetime, but through God's Grace, I am still standing.

No one deserves to live in constant upheaval, but the reality is that many people just like me experience abuse and violence in their own homes, at the hands of people whom they love. Living with an abusive person is basically conceding your peace to an exhausting succession of violence, tears, heartfelt apologies, and empty promises, only to stop for a little while and do it all over again. There are five stages of domestic abuse and each stage holds its own triumphs and challenges and when I really think about it, seems like I have spent my entire life cycling through those stages.

When I was a young girl growing up within my family I was in the first *honeymoon stage*. It was not perfect, but there was lots of laughter and good times. During the first honeymoon phase, everything *seemed* great. At the time I had no idea my experiences were setting the stage, or should I say a precursor to turmoil. As I reached my teen years I entered the *tension building phase* and things in my life began to spiral out of control. Stress and worry became a major part of my young life, and even though I was young, I could see the turbulence ahead, but I had no idea how to gain control. The majority of my young adult life was the *explosion*, and just like an eruption, everything blew up! There was destruction and a lot of things in my life died, figuratively.

After serving five years in prison, I went back to the *honeymoon phase*. Like my childhood, it was not perfect, but there was some laughter and good times as I tried to figure out this complicated thing we call life. Like I said before, the honeymoon phase has a way of fooling you into believing that everything is good, but it is really just camouflage for the dangers that lay underneath the surface. Thank God for growth and change, because in my 5th decade on this earth I am finally experiencing the *calm phase*; everything is finally lining up and I can exhale!! Thus far, my life has been a journey, but I wholeheartedly believe my steps have been ordered.

If you are reading my story and are experiencing abuse of any kind or living in a violent situation, please understand that you are not alone! I've read that God gives his toughest battles to the strongest soldiers, but I know this war is not one God intended for anyone! We are all precious in His sight, so we are worthy and deserving of a happily ever after ending! Living a joyful, contented life after abuse is possible and that is why I am sharing my story! This book is as much for my loved ones and the many wounded survivors whose stories reflect mine, as it is for me. I pray it reaches and teaches those who need it the most. Lord, let your will be done!

I call myself *The Grateful One* because many of the events in my life could've easily buried me, both figuratively and physically. But God saw fit to shower me with His Grace and Mercy and that lets me know there is purpose in my pain. Years ago I set out to find my WHY because I knew if I was going to survive this life and truly find happiness, I would have to go back and make some sense out of my existence.

So, this is me, starting over again…I admit, I've started over several times, but this time I think I've found the right formula. I've let go of what I thought I should have and embraced what God has given me. Instead of taking the broken pieces to my puzzle and burying them in the back yard, I am attempting to find exactly where each piece fits and how I can ease them into place without damaging them, or cutting myself and my loved ones on the sharp edges! I don't know if I will be able to complete the entire picture, but I do know I am willing to try.

Broken ideology is what molded me into one big ball of confusion and I have finally decided to step aside and let God work on me, but first I must peel back all the layers of trauma, and to do this I must dig up those sharp-edged puzzle pieces. Please understand, I am by no means an expert on trauma, but I have lived a great deal of my life in one state of upheaval or another, so I am confident that by sharing my story I can help others recognize the traumas in their lives and maybe stop it before it encompasses their entire being.

As a child of the seventies raised in the Deep South, I am a survivor of multiple traumas; some are identified and others so deeply embedded in the culture that they feel like an old comfortable robe. I believe it was those conflicts that influenced the way I viewed myself and life in general and ultimately led to my acceptance of physical, mental, and emotional abuse. While the memories are not easy to talk about and will absolutely hurt some people, I must speak on them for my own healing. It is my prayer that my experiences will save others from the harmful cycle of domestic abuse.

When I was growing up in the seventies, the mantra was, "It takes a village to raise a child" and while I wholeheartedly agree with the village concepts of being watchful, correcting undesirable behaviors when and where they occur, and protecting all children, whether they are yours or your neighbor's, I also know that every villager did not possess the values and moral fiber needed to raise well-rounded children. In fact, many of them were traumatized;

having been raised on the very same racist, primitive and dogmatic principles carried over generation after generation— dating all the way back to slavery.

In this instance, I am speaking specifically about the violence and mental abuse that doubled as punishment in many of our communities. From personal experience I can tell you, degrading remarks and frequent whippings can leave you broken and suffering from inferiority complexes that influence your behavior and alters your ability to make good choices. I know some people are saying "spare the rod and spoil the child," but we all know there is a difference between spanking and whipping. Spankings are corrective measures, and generally hurt your feelings more than anything; whereas whippings are intended to break your spirit and deter you from undesirable behaviors by injecting fear. Whippings are degrading. And when you don't feel good about yourself, you tend to accept people into your life who will misuse and treat you poorly. And honestly, sometimes we don't even recognize the trauma because the catalyst to that trauma is widespread and is generally accepted behavior because it started at home.

I was raised in the small, southeast Georgia community of Holmestown, which is a small area located within the city of Midway, Georgia. When I was growing up Holmestown was a quiet community of hard-working black families who cultivated and owned their land. The landscape consists of hundreds of land acreage scattered along the main stretch of Holmestown Road and about 3.5 miles of looping road, aptly called Holmestown Loop. There was a succession of single-family houses and mobile homes surrounded by huge, moss covered oak trees, and Georgia Pines. My family lived on the long stretch of highway leading into Holmestown in a nice, comfortable home that sat off the road to the left. We were situated on a piece of land that was owned by my maternal grandfather, Willie Hargrove, which also included his family home as well as my aunt Audrey's.

In our small community, everyone was acquainted and most of us were related in some fashion. My family practiced the Holiness religion and spent a lot of time in church and I believe many of our house rules were a direct result of what was taught in church. Children were to "speak when spoken to," and "do as

I say, not as I do," but I was a little bit different than most of the children I knew. Don't get me wrong, I wasn't a horrible child, but I was sassy and basically disregarded the rules that did not suit me. But believe me, my attitude landed me in a lot of trouble over the years, for my mama did not spare the rod.

My mama described me as a very stubborn and hardheaded child and I guess that is putting it mildly! I had a very independent spirit so I marched to the beat of my own drum. I had my own set of ideas and wasn't afraid to defiantly operate in them, even as a small child. I was always the one asking questions; I was the "but why" child who challenged authority. If it didn't look right to me, I called it out. I was never afraid to speak my mind. If *out of the mouth of babes* was a person, it definitely would have been me!

My parents, Arthur and Annie Golden, or Sonny and Mandy as they are known within the community, were no-nonsense, hardworking people who did their best to make sure we had food on the table and clothes on our backs. My parents married in 1962 when my mama was 14 years old and on more than one occasion my daddy has told me, come what may, he is committed to taking care of my mama until death do them part. And while the last 58 years have not been a bed of roses, God has blessed them with a long, productive union that has withstood through the best and truly the worst of times.

My parents' marriage bore six children, of which I am the third. I have two older siblings, a brother, Stephon, and my only sister, Cheryl, and three younger brothers Allen, Arthur, and my baby brother Alvin, whose completely unexpected birth brought our family total to eight. I was born on a scorching hot afternoon in August when the air was thick and the atmosphere was heavy with anger and grief, for I was born in 1968 and intense political and civil unrest in the United States of America.

At the time of my birth the country was embroiled in the Vietnam War; a conflict many African Americans did not support. 1968 was a particularly brutal year and many Americans died or were wounded through combat and non-combat related incidents in the jungles of Vietnam. It was a time when many black people unwillingly participated in a war abroad but also had to fight for equal rights domestically in a country that was built by our ancestors.

My birth in August came on the heels of the assassinations of Dr. Martin Luther King Jr. and Senator Bobby Kennedy, who had just made known his intentions to run for President in the upcoming election. While I do not know my parents' mindsets during that time, I dare say I was born of fierce passion, uncertainty, and emotional upheaval. Black people were angry at losing their leaders and the rioting that took place all over the country raged on for months thereafter. People were living day to day in turmoil and the entire country was in crisis.

Living in the confederacy I'm sure wasn't easy. I'm also certain that my parents experienced more than their share of emotional turmoil ranging from racism to trauma within the family structure that greatly influenced the way they lived and raised us. When you live in fear and oppression, and silence, generational curses will undoubtedly fester and flourish. Sadly, there are groups of people who have not been able to reverse or overcome the social damages fostered during those critical years. Like many other families, mine did not escape the collective dysfunction of our upbringing.

Combining the world's circumstances at the time of my birth with the fact that I was born under the astrological sign of Leo gives me a lot of insight into how some situations came to be in my life. Of course, I don't believe everything written about the zodiac, but truthfully, I cannot deny some of the traits as it pertains to my personality. A Leo's ruling element is fire and let's just say that is about right...I am strong, fiery, and passionate, but I can also be domineering and have a single-minded determination to succeed at a given task no matter what trials I might face in the pursuit! And that is not always a good thing because all accomplishments cannot be counted as successes.

When I say I am the epitome of a fierce Lioness, I mean it! But believe me when I can say those traits did not serve me well as a child, because my mama was just as determined to beat every bit of that fire out of me as I was committed to light up every room and situation with my presence, whether good or bad.

My relationship with my mother has always been complicated...At times it was a toxic co-dependency that landed us on opposite sides of the ring, anxiously awaiting the bell. But mostly, we have silently committed to maintaining some semblance of respect for one another because conflict is exhausting and oftentimes does not solve anything. While we have both committed unspeakable acts against each other over the years, today I respect the inherent strength in her and pray for her daily. She is one of the few people I know whose level of trauma matches (or exceeds) mine, so I don't harp on what could have been or what should have been and that is a true testament to my growth in God.

While my daddy was the head of our household, Mama was clearly the glue that held our family together and as such, we operated under her authority. Mama was raised in the church, but periodically throughout my upbringing, she would backslide, as the old folks say. And when she backslid, so did our family. When Mama was in her worldly persona, we were allowed to wear pants, and shorts, and experience freedoms that were normally unacceptable in our household. On the other hand, when she repented, all of our freedom went out the door right along with the pants and shorts and the changes were not up for debate! We were in church three nights a week come rain or shine.

As was common in those days, my mama rarely worked outside of the house unless she was going to help my grandmother in her little night club that was built on the property near my maternal grandparents' house. Both sets of my grandparents, Willie and Victoria Hargrove and Henry and Leola Golden lived nearby and were an ever-present part of our upbringing, so of course, there were rules on top of rules for me and my siblings. At some point during my childhood, Grandmama Leola suffered a mental breakdown and was institutionalized for the duration of her life, but Granddaddy did his best to support and help my parents raise us. Since Daddy worked on the railroad, Mama was the primary disciplinarian, and believe me when I say, she was tougher than any man! I was constantly being whipped for one reason or another.

I would be lying if I said I didn't deserve punishment because sometimes I did—probably most of the time. I knew there were consequence to my disobedience, but I was always the rebel of the bunch…Well, my younger brother Arthur was a pretty good rule breaker too, so let's just say he and I did what the others were either too smart or too afraid to do. Me and Arthur were mischievous and pushed the envelope on any type of boundaries that blocked our childish whims. When Mama said go right, oftentimes we went left! Needless to say, this did not bode well for my parents, who had their hands full raising six children during a time when defiance and disobedience could either land you in jail or worse, a cemetery. Mama was determined that the law would not have her children, so her punishment was quite often and plentiful for us when we were caught breaking any of the rules.

Mama did not spare the rod, the belt, switch, extension cord, or the broom handle when doling out punishment. I remember she would tell me in the midst of my whippings that she was trying to make me a better person and if I wasn't so hard-headed and stubborn that she wouldn't have to beat me so much. I guess she was trying to break me out of my defiant ways and I truly believe she thought whippings

15

would solve the problem. I have no doubt she only did what she knew to do. I believe she gave us what she was given, but that does not excuse the damage that was done.

Over time I seemed to develop an immunity to the whippings I suffered. Physical punishment became a part of my life that I did not like, but grew to accept and even expect. Whippings and name calling became steeped into my soul at a very young age and the damage it caused would show itself later on in some of the most critical times of my life.

I cannot speak definitively on my mother's mindset because I do not know a lot about her upbringing. However, I learned of a couple of incidents that took place both before and after marriage that I am sure traumatized my mama, but since she refuses to talk about it, I can only share my thoughts and feelings about how the trickle-down affected me. Although some of her actions over the years still make me question her love for me, please know that I love her unequivocally with the love of God; I have to believe she gave us all she had to give.

Even though I suffered whippings too numerous to count, I do not begrudge my childhood. At the time I thought it was normal and I felt lucky to have both of my parents living under one roof and caring for me and my siblings. We didn't want for much; my family thrived financially. We had all the trappings of success; a nice home, land, new cars, and plenty of food on the table thanks to Daddy's career choice. My daddy worked for the railroad company. He traveled all over the southeastern part of the country helping to modernize travel. Daddy was away from home during the week and would return home on the weekend, most of the time.

I loved it when he came home because things were much calmer and there was a lot of laughter around the house. Whenever we got into trouble, Daddy would try to defend me and Arthur and Mama always resented his input. She thought he was too lenient. I guess it seemed like he was rewarding our bad behavior because he would take us places with him; sometimes we would go to the store, fishing, or to check on our granddaddy at his farm. In hindsight, he was probably trying to give Mama a break from us! He didn't seem to mind how rambunctious we were and we are like the three amigos to this day.

I always felt more comfortable talking to my daddy about the important things in my life because he was always a little bit more open to my dreams. I was a little visionary; I fantasized about getting out of Holmestown and seeing the world. Even though Daddy did it through work, he traveled and met new people and I liked to pick his brain about his adventures. He would come home and tell us stories about the people he met on his travels and the different experiences he had working someplace new and it captivated me. Although we rarely traveled outside of Holmestown and Midway I wanted to explore the world and Daddy never discouraged my dreams.

Don't misunderstand me, my daddy is not perfect; neither of my parents are, but my relationship with my daddy is better than the one I share with my mama. I can remember times that they questioned each other's actions when it came down to the way they parented us. Mama thought daddy was too easy on us and to this day she still does not understand or like the dynamics of our relationship, but that is a story for another book. I have my own ideas about why, but I don't let it bother me anymore. My relationship with God assures me that His approval is my priority.

When I was younger I convinced myself that Mama's strict countenance was a result of the times and our religion. Given the climate of the country at the time of my birth, of course my family had strict rules in place to keep us safe. The Golden children were to be seen and not heard, always practice and show good manners, stay out of grown folks business, do our chores, not stray far away from home, obey all adults and stay in a child's place. However, the fiery little dreamer in me wanted to see, explore, and experience new things, so sometimes that included breaking a rule or two. While my older siblings weren't having any of that foolishness, oftentimes I dragged poor Arthur right along with me.

If you look at my siblings, physically we are like carbon copies of each other. We all share the same dark chocolate brown complexion, straight, proud nose, and slanted eyes, but our personalities couldn't be any more different. My two older siblings Steph and Cheryl are more refined; Steph is the oldest and he always took his big brother role seriously. He was and still is reliable, responsible, and just an all-around good guy. Cheryl was quiet; always studying and reading books, and not nearly as opinionated as I. Allen was a quiet, gentle soul who always kept to himself and still does to this day. In adulthood, my younger brother Alvin and I are like-minded in a lot of ways. We share the same work ethic and our personalities are similar, but growing up, he and the others did not try Mama as often as me and Arthur. I guess they knew the outcome of disobedience and chose not to be on the receiving end of Mama's punishment, which was always swift and uncompromising.

Aside from the harsh punishment, I was happy and proud to be a member of the Golden family! Ours was a huge close-knit circle and we shared lots of laughter and good times. I feel like some of my better qualities came from watching my dad's work ethic and because of the way he provided for our family in my formative years, I always looked for those qualities when choosing a mate. My mama, for all of her strict ways, was strong, and organized and she definitely taught me how to cook and take good care of the house. We had family barbecues and different events within the community that brought everyone out! My siblings, cousins, and I created our own fun; there were plenty of dirt roads and woods to explore in the neighborhood and we made the most of it.

We played softball, had relay races, and shared lots of laughter. Truthfully, with there being so many kids around, sometimes I just wanted to be seen. Having six children in the house, and so many extended family members around sometimes I felt like no one was really paying attention to me. So, on many occasions, I used the crowd to get away with mischief, but other times I made the crowd my stage and acted out because I wanted attention. The outcome was not always good, but that's just an example of the single-minded focus I possess. Sometimes the results are to my detriment.

Over the years I was punished a lot and the one thing I remember about Mama's whippings is they always ended with her saying that she loved me and just wanted me to be a better person. I don't question my punishments for the most part, because I was often

21

disobedient. I put myself in harm's way sometimes because I didn't see the need for some of the rules; I felt like they were too harsh and stifling. So, while I won't dispute the fact that I needed to be punished, I do take issue with the harsh types of discipline that I (and many of my generation) endured; the yelling, name-calling, and hitting with objects, mostly. It was too severe and caused generational suffering because hurt people tend to hurt other people. That's right, I said it! If you have a whole generation of damaged people raising children, what is the likelihood that those children won't be damaged, as well?

Some people will probably dispute my recollections because whippings were commonplace back then, but I have to speak *my* truth and in doing so, I have to call it what it is. And please understand I'm here to tell you about my story and my experience, so I am not speaking for anyone else. These memories are mine and mine alone. What I experienced as a child was abuse, plain and simple. And for those of you who doubt my word, please know I carry the receipts with me every day. As much as I would like to forget, the fact is, not only does my heart bear the weight of the abuse, my body bears the evidence; live and in living color.

While I hold no malice in my heart for my mother, I am putting all of my cards on the table. I only wish going into puberty I had a healthier view of abuse; what it really looked like, and what it entailed. I wish I knew that it was not acceptable and should not be a regular part of my everyday life. As a matter of fact, I wish we all had a healthier view of abuse; what it really looked like and what it entailed. I wish we knew that it was not acceptable and should not have been a regular part of everyday life. When you know better, you do better...But God knows I learned too late.

Book Two

Tension Building Phase

I can't recall the exact date, but I remember it was shortly after my 14th birthday that my life took a tragic turn. Well, let's go back a little bit further to 1980 because that is the year when all the trouble actually began. I was 12 years old on the night I crept out of my bedroom and sat down in the hallway eavesdropping on my parents and grandparents. They were in my family's living room trying to whisper amongst themselves, but because tensions were high and emotions had taken over, their words were urgent and just loud enough for me to hear a little bit of the conversation.

From my hiding place in the hallway, I could hear the anger in Daddy's voice; it seemed to shake the entire house when he spoke. In contrast, Mama's voice trembled a little bit when she responded, so I could tell she was nervous and I immediately knew something was wrong. I wasn't used to hearing uncertainty in Mama's voice; normally when she spoke, we knew she said what she meant and she meant what she said! So, to hear her voice shaking was alarming. She and Daddy had more than enough arguments for me to know that she was not easily intimidated and had no problem defending herself, but that night was different; she sounded frightened and it scared me.

As I cowered in the hallway I heard the words police and jail, and I remember Daddy's voice booming "Why did you take that knife?" The way he said those words scared the life out of me so bad that I started shaking. I was too scared to stand up, so I crawled quickly back to my bedroom and eased the door shut because I knew I had heard something that I was not supposed to hear. When I got on the other side of the bedroom door I realized I had been holding my breath and I exhaled quickly and took a few deep breaths. My heart was beating as if I ran the longest race of my life! I was so scared that I just sat there on the floor with my back against the door and cried silently in the dark. I did not understand what was going on, but I knew enough to know that my mama was in trouble. I sat on the floor for a long time listening to my heartbeat pounding in my ears. Sunlight was peeking through the curtains when I finally crawled back into bed.

I learned the details of that incident much later in life, but on the night it happened, I was confused about who had done what. All I knew was someone got stabbed and Mama was in some kind of trouble. As it turns out, the full story was actually worse than I imagined. By the time I awoke the next morning our family was in full crisis mode; everyone was crying because my mama had stabbed and killed a man. She said it was in self-defense, but she was arrested and charged with murder. The facts about that night have grown faint over time, so I can't give a lot of details but I can tell you this, Mama went to jail and from that point on, my life began a downward spiral.

There were too many unanswered questions and so much sadness in our house for the next few days. I didn't know how long my mama would be away and the adults wouldn't tell us anything because of course, it was grownup's business. I wanted to ask Daddy and Grandmama questions, but somehow, I knew it was not the right time for me to be Miss Inquisitive so I kept my mouth shut. I'm sure they were too busy trying to figure out what they could do to help bring Mama home, anyway.

I can't say exactly how long Mama initially stayed in jail, but it seems like it was just a few days before she was released on bond. While she wasn't away for a long time, it was long enough to give me a glimpse of what life would be like without her in it consistently and I did not like it. Mama was a hard taskmaster and we constantly butted heads, but I can honestly say it was her presence that gave me stability and kept me from going completely astray because Daddy was gone so often. Never mind, he was not much of a disciplinarian anyway, so needless to say when she was not present, disorder ensued in our household. I always resented Mama's rules and all of the punishment I constantly received, but when she was gone I didn't even enjoy my freedom because I was too busy praying for hers.

After she was released on bond, Mama returned home to await her trial. In the interim, we reverted back to our household norms, even though it seemed like my parents had more arguments and we spent more time at my grandparents' houses. The dynamic between me and my mama changed for a little while because I was happy to have her home, so I stayed close by and followed the rules. Nevertheless, as time went on, things went back to normal and we began butting heads even more so, because I was going through puberty and "smelling myself," as the old folks say. But I was still happy that she was home because things were changing with my body and I was becoming curious about the opposite sex. I really needed her guidance more than ever!

When Mama got arrested I understood a lot better why all of the rules were needed in the first place; trouble is easy to find, and sometimes you don't have to go looking for it because people will bring it to your doorstep. That is exactly what happened to my mama; she became a victim of the very same lesson she tried to teach me.

I began my freshman year of high school in the fall of 1982. I attended the local high school, Bradwell Institute in nearby Hinesville and was learning to navigate my way around the campus, which was twice the size of my old middle school. So many things about high school were different from middle school — namely, I was now a lowly freshman, whereas in my last year of middle school I was the upperclassman. At BI, as they called my high school there were over a thousand students! I was amazed by the large crowds and the upperclassmen looked and acted like adults! It was a whole new world for me so I made sure to stick close to my sister and the people from my community for guidance.

In October, we celebrated Homecoming, and I thoroughly enjoyed the festivities that accompanied the weekend. I loved the different events and celebrations throughout the year, and it all started with Homecoming. We had a hall decorating contest between the classes and a dance after the football game to start the Homecoming weekend off! There was so much excitement in the air and everything seemed to be moving in a positive direction for me.

I was excited about life and though Mama and I continued to butt heads, I found solace in being able to periodically escape to my Grandfather's farm, which was located within a half-mile of our home.

Granddaddy had a huge farm with land acreage that extended farther than the eyes can see. He had fruit trees that lined the property and a huge garden full of fresh vegetables that always seemed ripe for picking. Whenever we would finish our chores around the house, Mama allowed us to walk to Granddaddy's house to spend the rest of the day. We loved going to the farm because there was so much room for us to roam freely and I loved picking fresh fruit off the trees and exploring the grounds. I especially liked witnessing new growth in the gardens.

In November of that year, my family had the usual large family celebration for the Thanksgiving holiday. There was plenty of food, laughter, and guests who stopped by our house. We had a short vacation from school for Thanksgiving Break, but like most young people I looked forward to Christmas and the longer two-week break we had coming. I wish I could say I was excited by all the things I was learning in the classroom but that was not the case. I was more excited about social activities, and of course the Christmas presents. I already knew what I wanted, which was for my daddy to give me money so I could buy some new clothes.

By the time the holidays rolled around, I was comfortable in high school; I knew my way around and met a lot of new people in my classes. Life was good and my teen years were shaping up nicely. I noticed the older girls wearing a lot of new, trendy clothes and I planned to purchase a pair of Calvin Klein jeans and some stirrup pants because they looked cute with leg warmers and oversized sweatshirts. We were going through one of those times when we were allowed to wear jeans, so I wanted to take full advantage! I definitely needed new shoes to wear with my new clothes and I wanted to get my hair done over the break. I had regular, everyday teenage issues on my mind, so my thoughts were far removed from the incident that happened with my mama. In fact, the week after Thanksgiving made almost two years that a man died at my mama's hands, and sadly enough it was also the point that time ran out for my family.

We found out the following week that Mama's trial for murder would begin and my family was devastated. It seemed like the bad news just popped up out of nowhere; one day I was enjoying high school and the next day I was faced with the possibility that my mama would be going away for a very long time, and it just didn't seem fair! I'm sure my parents knew about the pending trial, but I had no idea it was happening; maybe they wanted us to enjoy what could be our last family holiday together. It just didn't seem real.

So much time had passed that I somehow pushed the thought of her going to prison to the back of my mind. In my young intellect, I thought they must have either forgotten about the incident or decided to let Mama go because she said she killed him in self-defense. In a conversation I had with my mama some years after she returned home, she told me that she was out so long that even she had begun to doubt that she was going to prison, but we were both wrong.

On December 1, 1982, my mama was convicted of felony murder of a man from our community named Peter Robertson, Jr. During the trial several things came out about the events leading up to the incident. According to court records, the night my mama killed Mr. Robertson, he came to our house drunk earlier that day while my daddy was home. He accused my mama of infidelity. The court records do not indicate with whom he had accused her of cheating, but court testimony does indicate that he drank a lot and was somewhat of a troublemaker in the community, and surely that was what he was doing when he came to our home to inform my daddy about my mama's alleged indiscretions.

After Mr. Robertson left our house that day court records state that my parents got into a really bad argument, which I am sure angered and embarrassed Mama. Later on that night, my mama took a kitchen knife with her when she went to my grandmama's club. Court records say Mr. Robertson followed Mama to the club and continued to make accusations. Mama threw a drink in his face, and she said in her testimony that he made a move towards her and she stabbed him in the chest in self-defense. Witnesses testified that he did not make a move towards her; they said Mama stabbed him in the midst of the argument from across the bar. The jury convicted Mama of Felony murder and sentenced her to life in prison. Because no appeal was forthcoming she did not return home for many, many years.

Mama's conviction was the worst thing that could have happened to me and my family; it literally tore us apart. I constantly worried with her being away from us. Not only was I concerned about her, but I also had my worries that flooded my mind constantly. What were the people in the community saying about her? What were they saying about our family because we were good people! I worried about what the people in the church had to say and I could not even imagine what my daddy was going to do without Mama? What was going to happen to us with daddy being gone all weeklong? My mama's incarceration and the subsequent family crisis that arose thereafter was the first of many traumatic events that occurred in my young life.

After my mama left, life as I knew it changed drastically! Our family unit was shattered. It seemed as if time literally stood still day after day. For a while, everyone moped around; we were either crying excessively or eerily quiet. The uncertainty of what would follow affected us all in different ways. There were so many unanswered questions floating around in my young mind that sometimes I had to pray for sleep just to quiet the voices. How long will she be away? Who is going to make sure we eat and how is the household going to run without Mama laying down the law? Daddy's job already had him away from the house during the week, but Mama's absence kept him away from home even more. We started to see less and less of him. Without Mama's presence, it no longer felt like a home and the sad reality was from that point on, our home was irretrievably broken.

Yes, I was always getting into trouble and being accused of all manner of things by my mama, but I soon came to realize that her presence fostered a sense of security for me. The relationship we shared — however toxic some elements were, kept me safe and contained the dangerous little fire down on the inside of me. And truth be told, I suffered without her guidance. Mama provided the day to day routine; she made sure we ate, bathed, did our chores, and were held accountable. Those were things I never thought much about when I was moaning and groaning about the rules I found so restricting. Needless to say, it was a wakeup call but it was too late. Mama was gone and I did not know which way to turn.

As for Daddy, he was overwhelmed and I imagine coming home to a house without his wife and six sad children was a lot for him to deal with, so as time went on, my daddy, who was always my hero, checked out on our family. Rumor had it that he was seeing a lady in our community who lived not too far from us. I guess his new relationship was what Daddy needed to make him forget about his wife in prison and his six grieving children. Everyone in the community knew about their involvement. It wasn't hidden and that made it even worse. I really looked up to my daddy and for a long time afterward, I was angry with him and felt abandoned. I do not know what he was dealing with, I just know he was not there with us, and our new normal involved a lot of freedom that I had asked for, but definitely was not ready to receive.

When Mama went to prison, her mother, Grandmama Victoria, stepped in to raise us. My parents had six children ranging from ages eight to 18, so Grandmama Victoria had her hands full feeding, clothing, and taking care of us. She did the best she could to keep us in line and believe me it was no easy task. We all suffered emotionally, but were expected to just push through, and for the most part, we did. We carried on and continued to live even though we were dying inside. She did her best to keep us together and provide some stability, but it was a lot for Grandmama to handle. Me, Steph, and Cheryl were basically left to our own devices because we could pretty much tend to our day to day needs, but my three younger brothers needed constant care and guidance. Keep in mind, all of us were traumatized, as I am sure my grandmother was as well. She lost her daughter with whom she shared a close relationship to prison, and as a mother, I cannot imagine the sense of loss she suffered, not to mention the transition of household duties.

Some days Grandmama Victoria bent, but she did not break, because we were truly the walking wounded and she knew we needed her! None of us handled Mama's incarceration well, but my younger brothers Allen and Arthur became extremely rebellious. They kept Grandmama on her toes! Alvin had a hard time dealing with Mama's absence too, but instead of acting out, he withdrew into himself because that was his way of coping. We were all forced to grow up very quickly, which both excited and scared me at the same time.

By the time Mama left, I was already sneaking around with boys doing adult stuff. I thought I was a grown woman, but when reality set in that I was truly responsible for myself, all of that bravado went out the window! For many years I wished I didn't have anyone telling me what to do but when it actually happened I quickly got a bitter taste of adulthood that I did not like.

I tried to cover up my devastation by being extra loud, extra happy, and just plain extra! I was everywhere; the local recreation department, the park, or just hanging out. If there was a crowd, I was there! I enjoyed socializing with my brothers and cousins, playing softball, and trying to be grown. I was sexually active and you could not tell me I was not a grown woman. I was handling adult duties trying to help my siblings maintain our household as well, but underneath all of the boldness lay a broken young girl who just wanted her family back.

Less than a year after my mama went to prison, I went to play softball in a park in Hinesville. It was a few days before my 15th birthday and I was kind of excited to see if anyone would remember my birthday with all that occurred over the last year. When the game wrapped up, everyone left and went their separate ways before I had an opportunity to ask anyone for a ride. I found myself alone in the park, so I began walking towards home.

It was a long walk, but I figured someone I knew would eventually come along and give me a ride. As I walked down Memorial Drive a car passed by headed in the opposite direction. The driver turned around and slowed down beside me and asked where I was going. I glanced over at him and noticed he was cute, so I stopped walking and stood sassily with my hand on my hip. I can't remember a lot about his features because over the years I blocked him out of my mind, but I do recall that he was dark-skinned, kind of young and as I said before, really cute. I was surprised that he stopped to talk to me because I was hot and sweaty, and my hair was standing up all over my head from playing a long game of softball, but that didn't seem to matter to him. I was so excited I could barely contain myself, so when he asked if I wanted a ride, I jumped at the chance. I ran around to the passenger side and got in the car, thankful that I didn't have to walk all the way home in the heat.

After exchanging names, I told him to go straight and take a left on Highway 84. We headed east and rode with the windows down in the car, enjoying the breeze that was blowing. In hindsight, you could not have convinced me there was anything wrong with what I had done by getting into the car with a complete stranger. I was young and fearless, and being in that car made me feel good; I felt like a cool grownup. I was sitting in the passenger seat unknowingly riding towards my next trauma and all I was thinking about was how lucky I was that he stopped to talk to me!

He turned up the music as we headed down the highway. I felt so light and carefree sitting in the passenger seat of that strange man's car. It felt worlds away from my messed-up life and for a moment I just felt happy. As we approached McLarry's Curve he slowed down and turned left, headed towards the back gate to Fort Stewart. Earlier, when I got in the car, he told me he was in the Army and had been in the area for a few months, so I knew he lived on the military base, but I had not agreed to go back to his room, so I was wondering where he was taking me.

I looked over at him, and as if he was reading my mind, he glanced at me with a crooked smile and told me we were going out to the pond for a little while and get to know each other. It's funny how some details are so vivid, but obviously, I blocked out other parts of my ordeal because I don't remember anything about his features, except his smile. I specifically remember his smile because for some reason when he did it, I thought that smile was just for me. I was flattered, so I smiled back and nodded my head that it was cool. He seemed like the type of guy I would love to get to know and my excitement grew as we slowed down and took a right onto a little dirt road that led to Holbrook Pond.

It turns out he had much more in mind than getting to know each other. When we came into the clearing there was a beautiful, huge pond with a deck. It was surrounded by trees and a couple of picnic areas and I imagined us walking on the deck holding hands. He parked the car close to the wood line and leaned over to kiss me. Before long we were fully engaged and he was taking off my shirt. He was on top of me and things started moving very fast. Everything happened so quickly that I barely had time to react. I got scared and wanted to stop because I was feeling overwhelmed, but he would not stop. I felt degraded and very, very stupid.

Afterwards, he apologized. He said he thought I wanted it because I got into his car so easily and when we arrived at the pond I did not reject his kisses. And he was right, I didn't. I kissed him back because I wanted him to like me. I wanted to walk around the pond and hold hands while we talked. I wanted him to get to know me. If I knew that kissing him back would lead to rape, I would not have done it, but it's all water under the bridge. I was young and inexperienced, and I didn't know any better, but I quickly learned about consequences and repercussions.

I asked him to take me home and after reassuring him numerous times that I would not tell anyone what happened, he dropped me off in front of my house. I never saw him again; thankfully not even in the face of my son who was born nine months later. Grandmama was not at our house when I arrived home, so I did not have to tell her what happened to me that day. I locked myself in my bedroom and cried myself to sleep that night and many nights thereafter. I could not believe I was so dumb!

I can say a lot of things about that incident, as it is yet another sharp-edged piece to my puzzle that I chose to hide for many years. Even when people said ugly and vile things about me being pregnant at a young age, I chose to omit that incident. Even as people around me guessed at the origin of my pregnancy, and made nasty comments and horrible accusations against me, I chose to tell only those who I felt needed to know because I was terribly ashamed of myself and had begun judging myself very harshly. How dare I think that a guy that good looking was really interested in me? Never mind he was a rapist and likely a repeated sexual predator, my lack of self-worth would not allow me to blame him for what happened.

I blamed myself for the rape and after it happened I descended to a low, dark, and scary place; I was a bundle of nerves. It seemed like bad things were always happening in my life and I did not understand what I had done to deserve all the horror I was suffering. I had no self-esteem, but I hid it behind a wall of laughter and jokes, but deep down I knew I was on the wrong path.

When I discovered I was pregnant...Well, when my grandmama *told me* I was pregnant, I was shocked! I knew I was not feeling normal, but since my cycle was irregular, I never considered that I could be pregnant. I was only fifteen years old and I had no idea what to look for anyway. I was so confused! I was pregnant, my daddy had another family and was making pit stops home every now and then and my mama was in prison. My grandmama did her best to help with my care and help me make decisions about my future, but I was too busy trying to find a way to cope with everything I was dealing with in the present to even think into the future. I had no idea what to expect.

My pregnancy was not a happy time for me. I experienced many moments of anguish and hopelessness because I had no idea what I was going to do with a baby. I was living my life day by day trying to figure it out one minute at a time, in between bouts of loneliness. I thought about my mama often and I knew if she was there I would have probably been in big trouble for putting myself in a position to be raped, but afterward, she would have made sure I was taken care of. On second thought, I probably would not have been in the park in Hinesville in the first place because Mama didn't play about us being too far away from home. But Mama was not there and her absence was more pronounced during my pregnancy.

I didn't understand the things that were happening with my body. In retrospection, they were common symptoms of pregnancy, but I was too young and inexperienced to know what to expect. The sickness, fatigue, and cravings had me confused and then there were times when I would have flashbacks and relive the trauma of my rape. Sometimes that crooked smile would wake me up out of my sleep and other times I would be going about my day when suddenly

I could literally feel his hands holding me down. Other times I could hear his voice apologizing over and over again, telling me that he thought I wanted it. I stopped trusting people and for a while, I became angry and combative with my family.

I now recognize that not only was my hormones raging, but I suffered from Post-Traumatic Stress Disorder and no one knew what I was going through. I was a complete mess. I was in the 10th grade, barely going to school. I had no education, no job, and no idea how to start planning for a baby. I spent the majority of the time going back and forth between trying to figure out how I was going to take care of a baby and pretending that I was not pregnant at all.

My grandmama tried, but she really did have her hands full with taking care of her home and raising my younger brothers. Allen and Arthur were still having a hard time dealing with all of the changes and acted out to the point where Grandmama let them come and stay at home with us older siblings. My daddy was absent most of the time and when he was around I was not trying to talk to him anything because I was disappointed in him and disappointed in myself too.

I felt like my life was on a fast track to nowhere, so I stopped going to school and eventually dropped out. I didn't want to hear what my peers were saying about me, anyway. People can be so judgmental and cruel sometimes. Instead of mocking and ridiculing each other, we should take time to learn what others are dealing with and be a blessing instead of judge and jury, but I digress. It was my path to walk.

I imagined that everybody thought I was just a fast-tailed little girl who got knocked up, so I stayed home and sat around feeling sorry for myself. As I got bigger, my self-esteem got smaller. I was depressed and it seemed like no one could get through to me, not that there were a lot of people trying. It was almost as if everyone expected me to just handle it, so I somehow did. When I finally accepted the fact that my baby was coming I turned to God because I didn't feel like I had any other help. Like the old folks say, I made my bed hard, so I laid in it.

My growing belly made me realize I had another life to take care of, so I started seeking and praying incessantly to God for a way out of the mess my life had become. I drew strength from the biblical teachings I learned over the years when we spent three nights a week in church. Oh, how I hated it when we had to do it, but thank God when I needed the word, it was tucked away in my heart. My grandmama talked to me tirelessly about looking to the hills and making the best out of a bad situation, and while I did not understand completely back then, I trust that it was her prayers that kept me.

I don't know where I would be if I didn't have Missionary Victoria Hargrove, my grandmama! She was the rock that held us down when the storm winds blew. I really regretted being disobedient and landing myself in all of that trouble because whatever affected me, affected her. She was already charged with the heavy load of her daughter's children, but to add a baby to her already full plate was a lot to carry. I'm in awe of the strength she possessed to hold our family together during that time, but she somehow managed through the Grace of God. As much as I went through, I was blessed in my relationship with Grandmama and I thank her for teaching me how to pray and for petitioning God on my behalf when I was pregnant and felt like I was alone in the world.

After much prayer and preparation, I focused on finding the positive things that arose after being violated in such a careless manner. I chose to concentrate on my baby, who was having a field day moving around in my stomach. The feeling of new life and the opportunity to make my baby's life better than mine encouraged me greatly. At the time it was a hard pill to swallow, but something good eventually arose from the ashes of my ordeal! Had I not gone through that bad encounter, I would not be able to experience the gift of unconditional love I receive from my first born, who is one of my biggest supporters and mirrors me in too many ways to mention.

My son, Deville was born on May 6, 1984 a few months shy of my 16th birthday. He was the spitting image of me and for that I was grateful. Between me and my grandmama we found a way for me to get through all that had occurred, but I was still living day by day. Every day held its trials with me trying to raise a baby when I was just a baby myself, but we somehow got through. I struggled financially, emotionally, and spiritually, but I got up every day and tried to put on a happy face, but it wasn't easy. I made it a point to say my prayers every night before I slept, no matter what, because I desperately needed a way out.

My way out came in the form of a 28-year-old soldier named Alfredo Gonzalez. We met one night when my sister and her boyfriend set us up on a blind date. We went out to eat dinner and from that day we were inseparable. We did everything together for the next few months. Alfredo stepped in and provided everything I was missing; stability, love, and financial resources. I had just given birth to my son a few months prior to meeting him and absolutely was not at my best. I was still carrying extra weight from my pregnancy, I was young, and confused and had a second mouth to feed. Alfredo took such great care of us that I could only surmise that he was the way out I had prayed for; he was a Godsend.

Alfredo professed his love for me after dating for only a few weeks and when he asked me to be his wife a few months later, I felt like I had died and gone to heaven. I was a 15-year-old single mother before he came along and I felt incredibly trapped inside of my life. I literally felt helpless most days; like my life was never going to change. Naturally, when Alfredo asked me to be his wife, I jumped at the chance. I didn't think about anything else except how he made me feel. For the first time in a long time, I felt like someone cared about me and made me a priority.

We didn't have to ask my daddy for permission to get married because Alfredo had already researched and found out that we could marry without parental consent in South Carolina. Truthfully, it probably would not have mattered anyway because I was a liability for my family. Me and my son were two extra mouths to feed and my marriage gave Daddy and Grandmama two less people to worry about given the circumstances. I thought it was a win, win situation for everybody, but believe me, if I had any idea of the troubles that lay ahead, I would have run to the farthest corner of the universe to avoid the heartbreak in my path.

Alfredo and I drove to Ridgeland, South Carolina on a cool, crisp Saturday morning in December 1984 and married at the local courthouse. I thought all of my problems were behind me because I had a husband to love and provide for me and Deville. Alfredo moved us into Denmark Trailer Park, a little mobile home community outside of the back gate to Fort Stewart and we began our life as husband and wife. In the beginning, things were great! We had a lot of good times and laughter in that little trailer, but it did not last because the façade my husband built around himself started to crumble as his drinking increased and our social life became more active.

It started innocently enough; my husband eased me back into abuse little by little with actions so familiar to me that I didn't even realize it was happening. In hindsight, some things began before we got married, but I had so many stars in my eyes that I didn't notice. Even if I had been living in a stable environment I probably would not have recognized what was happening because I was fifteen years old when Alfredo began grooming me and despite all of my bravado, I didn't have much experience with men or the world outside of my small community. Alfredo's attention flattered me. He picked out and purchased all of my clothing and shoes and showed me how to dress and behave to please him. It made me feel special that he loved me enough to marry me, and not just have sex, as guys my age did. So, when he made any special requests, I was more than happy to comply.

In the beginning, I felt privileged that Alfredo invested time and money to help me become a better person. I was young and inexperienced and had a lot of trauma in my life, so I didn't think a lot of people wanted to be bothered with me and all of my baggage. I was extremely grateful when God blessed me with Alfredo; my eyes were full of stars, so I could not see anything except what was right in front of me. I had a husband and a home to call my own. Alfredo was a great provider, so I didn't have to count on my family to help me financially. I thought my marriage had stopped me from being another young, black, single mother on welfare, but in retrospect, I would have much preferred to become that statistic as opposed to the one I became in my marriage.

Hindsight is 20/20, so now I can clearly see that all of the attention Alfredo gave to me and the care he took in making sure I was dressed properly and had everything I needed was just a prelude to what was coming. Abusers often camouflage their controlling ways under the guise of concern and care for their victims. I did not have anyone to shop for me or take time to pick out clothes just for me, so I appreciated every bit of the attention Alfredo poured into me. Whether he was buying me clothes or telling me how he wanted me to walk, sit, or speak, I was grateful and thought the sun rose and set on my man! I embraced his attention because at the time I desperately needed it and I truly thought we were in love.

It had been so long since I felt like someone genuinely paid attention to me and there was no way I was going to jeopardize the life we were building together. I was committed to doing whatever it took to make sure our marriage was successful, whether good or bad. As far as I was concerned, I had escaped a bad situation; my marriage to Alfredo saved me. Our marriage made me respectable and Deville had a mother and father to love him. I did not have to ask my family for anything because Alfredo provided well for us. I felt safe and for the first time in a long time I had security, so I did what I had to do to keep it that way. That included allowing my husband to have complete control over me and our life.

Book Three

The Explosion

I was seventeen years old when I finally admitted that something was terribly wrong with my marriage. Alfredo's controlling ways had gotten out of hand and it bothered me more and more every day. Truth be told, I started noticing some troubling behavior months into our marriage, but I did not let on that it bothered me for fear that Alfredo would leave and we would end up back in Holmestown with my family. I had grown weary of the jealous outbursts and verbal abuse, but I convinced myself that it wasn't so bad. At least he wasn't putting his hands on me.

I was accustomed to being called out of my name because that was one of the weapons my mama used against me. I did not like it, but it was a common occurrence. Hearing it come out of my husband's mouth admittedly did sting a bit more than it did during my childhood, because he was my husband and I wanted to please him and have his respect. Nevertheless, I endured because Alfredo always found a way to blame me for his abusive behavior. According to him, *he loved me so much and just wanted me to be a better wife and mother.* Like my mother, he said I was hard-headed, so I tried even harder to be compliant to his demands.

Early on in the marriage, he began alienating me from my family; Alfredo did not like me being around anyone unless he was present. He definitely did not like me in the company of other men, whether he was a family member or not, yet he would be the one who invited his male friends into our home. To keep me in line, Alfredo gave me backhanded compliments or made cruel jokes about my looks that hurt my feelings and made me feel insecure. When I complained he told me I had nothing to complain about because he was taking care of me and I did not want for anything.

Petty name-calling eventually led to outright criticisms and insults. He would call me fat and ugly and say no one wanted me except him and for a long time I believed him because I did not view myself in a positive light. I had low self-esteem for years and never really believed I had a lot to look forward to or offer. I was Alfredo's wife and Deville's mother, but other than that I did not see myself as anything more and my husband used my low self-esteem to make me feel unworthy of love from others and I admit, I fell for it.

As time went on, I started thinking about how my new life was starting to mirror my old life and I began to feel trapped again. Alfredo did not want me to have friends and he would act out if I invited people to come to our house. He invited whomever he wanted since he was paying all the bills, and there was nothing I could do except deal with it. My husband did not think my feelings mattered and eventually, I got tired of being overlooked and treated poorly, so I told Alfredo I was leaving. At first, he laughed and told me to go back to my miserable life; I would see that no one wanted me around. Of course, I believed him, but at that point, I did not care what he said or what anyone thought; I just wanted to leave, so I packed our things to go. When he realized his words didn't faze me, and I was still determined to leave, Alfredo became angry and abusive and that is when the physical violence began.

The first time he hit me, I fought back, but I was no match for Alfredo's anger. While he was beating me, he told me I was his property and I wasn't going anywhere until he said so. He called me ungrateful and that upset me terribly because I was doing everything he asked of me and it still wasn't enough. I was so hurt and angry and I wanted to keep fighting back, but the combination of Alfredo's physical strength and ugly words penetrated my soul and I was defeated.

Deep down inside I knew it was going to happen eventually, but I don't think a person can ever be prepared for that kind of violence coming from someone they love. After the first fight, his aggression towards me became more frequent. Sometimes I did not have to do anything to catch his wrath; it came with his mood swings. One minute he would be laughing and joking and next thing you know, a black mood would come over him and he would turn into a different person.

My husband had two sides; the one that was very sociable and enjoyed entertaining guests often collided with the jealous one who forbade me to be around other men. When that happened, things were extremely bad for me. Alfredo would invite his friends over to party and drink and after they left he would accuse me of flirting with someone and the beatings would commence.

For almost two years I endured a vicious cycle of beatings, heartfelt remorse, tears, apologies, and empty promises to never do it again. I became a prisoner in my home, tiptoeing around so I would not anger him. This cycle went on until I became pregnant with *our* first child together. For the duration of the time I carried our daughter, Alfredo did not hit me at all. It was like a lightbulb went off inside of his head and he realized that by hitting me he could potentially harm his daughter; never mind the damage he was doing to someone else's daughter.

Alfredo was ecstatic about his pending fatherhood. His face would light up when I walked into the room with my growing belly. He looked forward to our daughter's birth, so he handled me very carefully. I don't really know what aspect of my pregnancy brought about the change, but I was grateful for the reprieve because before the pregnancy I had been frequently on the receiving end of Alfredo's rage. I had grown tired of all of the control and had started speaking up for myself and he did not like it at all. Because I was challenging Alfredo, our fights had gotten worse and I knew they would soon reach a breaking point.

Our daughter Ashley was born on June 3, 1986, just three days before my classmates at Bradwell Institute graduated from high school. I should have been there, but I left school years ago and had not looked back. On what would have been my graduation day, I was returning home from the hospital with my 2nd child; my life was far removed from my classmates' and it was more pronounced than ever on that day. My daughter was beautiful; physically she was the spitting image of her father and Alfredo was overjoyed. For a couple of months longer, things were great because my husband was absolutely in love with our little girl.

For a while, we seemed like a normal family, albeit I was 17 years old and the mother of two small children, but I was also a teenager who longed to have friends to talk to and socialize with. I did not have a job and sitting in the house with two children all day long was taking a toll on my mental health. I wanted to hang out sometimes and live a normal life with regular teenage conversations but Alfredo's jealousy made that almost impossible because no one wanted to be a part of our family drama.

I began to rebel against him by going out and trying to meet new friends but my newfound independence and defiant behavior only resorted in more frequent beatings. Over the next year, I left Alfredo several times, but he would always come and find me. I was not safe anywhere, not even amongst my family. I remember packing up my children and going to Holmestown on different occasions, but my family did not freely welcome me because they knew wherever I went, Hurricane Alfredo would soon follow. They were unwilling to put themselves in harm's way for me, so I always ended up going back.

I can't say that I blame my family because Alfredo's foolishness was a lot to deal with and I was just as confused. I was on that dysfunctional roller coaster ride right along with Alfredo. I didn't want to live with the abuse, but sometimes in my dysfunction, I chose abuse over struggling by myself. I truly wanted to raise my children in a two-parent home like I was raised, but I have come to realize that there is no benefit in raising children in financial stability when there is no mental and emotional constancy.

I wish I had someone back then who would have stood up for my children, if not for me. I was 18 years old and my emotional maturity level was underdeveloped. I believed I was grown because I was handing grown folk's responsibilities, but inside I was a child raising children. Playing an adult role made my bed hard over time, but I never realized how hard it actually was until I tried laying in it. I just wish my children did not have had to lay in it with me because I knew eventually if nothing changed, it would become my deathbed.

I became pregnant with my third child in the midst of the turmoil I was going through with my husband. During that pregnancy, Alfredo tormented me almost daily! Ashley was only four months old when we conceived our son, so I do not know if he was not yet ready for another child or what motivated him to be more abusive towards me, but it seemed like he was always angry with me. I was subjected to the worst abuse ever, both physically and mentally. I left a couple of times, but it was a burden on my family, so each time I ended up going back. I honestly do not know how I was able to carry my baby to term, except by the Grace of God.

Alfredo Jr., or Freddie as we call him was born on July 31, 1987, 13 months after I gave birth to Ashley. I wish I could say it was a happy time for me, but it was not, and what affected me, also affected my baby. During my pregnancy with Freddie, I was stressed out and cried a lot because of Alfredo's abuse, and in turn, Freddie cried a lot, which aggravated Alfredo even more. But in the midst of being beat down, I finally became strong enough to leave for an extended period. I realized that Alfredo was not emotionally capable of taking care of me and our family and I knew if I continued to stay and take the abuse it would become my life and, ultimately, my children's lives as well. Deville, Freddie, and Ashley were innocent children and they deserved to be safe and protected. Thankfully, Alfredo's wrath was never directed towards them; he just did not spare their mother.

The first few days after fights were usually the best times to have serious discussions because we would go back to the honeymoon phase and Alfredo would be very remorseful and apologetic. So, one morning after a particularly violent fight the night before I asked Alfredo why he wanted me around when he obviously did not love me. When I questioned his love for me, he looked at me like I was crazy. He said "Vicky, don't I work every day and take care of you? Don't I provide a roof over your head and make sure everybody in this house eats?" I told him yes, because he did provide for us. He paid all the bills and made sure we were taken care of, just like my daddy did for our family growing up. Alfredo looked at me and said "That *is* love, Vicky! Taking care of my family is love!" I pondered that for a while; I thought about all the whippings I received as a child and how my mama would tell me while hitting me that she loved me and wanted me to be a better person. That was the only kind of love I knew, but it was not good enough. I realized that by marrying Alfredo I had not put myself in a better place; I had simply replaced my parents with my husband, and why not? I was a child with a limited capacity to make sound adult decisions. The realization shocked me! I was just cycling through the same type of treatment and behaviors with a different perpetrator, but I also realized I did not want to live the rest of my life that way.

I concluded that Alfredo had no idea what I needed and he was never going to provide a safe home for me and our children. At that point, I just wanted some peace in my life and to achieve it I would have to leave our home because my husband did not think there was an issue with the way we lived. I found out years later that Alfredo had his own demons. His anger and rage resulted from his father's abusive and dismissive behavior towards his own family.

When he was twelve years old Alfredo found out from a chance meeting with a boy who looked just like him, that his father had another family who lived in the same city, just several blocks from their home. As a result, he grew up believing that he was not enough. His father provided for both families very well, but emotionally, my husband was untrusting, angry, and deprived. He was an angry child who grew up to be an abusive adult.

When I found out about his past, my heart went out to him. I understood more about why Alfredo behaved the way he did, but I could not accept his abusive treatment. My mama's whippings damaged my self-esteem and almost broke my spirit, but I was never scared for my life. Alfredo's type of love injected fear into my entire being and that was something I was not willing to accept.

That morning, I made the decision to leave for good and I was determined not to return come hell or high water. I applied for subsidized housing and waited anxiously until an apartment became available before I made my move. It took a few months, but just knowing that I had a plan in place gave me a sense of peace. I am sure Alfredo suspected something because calm had overcome me, but I never let on that I was leaving. He just came home one day and I was gone. My children and I moved into our little apartment and I tried to build a normal life for them although my husband stalked and harassed me almost daily.

Inevitably, he caused so much disruption and problems at my home that I was given multiple warnings and finally evicted after he broke into my apartment and vandalized it beyond recognition. He punched holes in the walls, slashed my living room furniture, and turned over tables and chairs. He ruined all of my clothing and caused thousands of dollars in damages, leaving me and my children destitute.

We went to stay with my family, but Alfredo immediately came after us. When my daddy met him at the door, my husband told him that he did not want to disrespect him, but I was his wife and he did not have a problem going through him to get to me. Daddy told me I had to go with my husband because he did not want any trouble in his home. So having nowhere else to go, I ended up back with Alfredo, subjected to his wrath. I no longer had any love for him and I wanted to remove my children from that abusive situation before they became old enough to know what was going on or he began physically abusing them too. I prayed about it and started making plans to leave again. Permanently.

I began saving money little by little so when I left the next time I would have at least enough to rent a place to stay since I knew he would follow me to Holmestown. I had been evicted, so I was not eligible to move into subsidized housing again. I had to find a job that paid well enough for me to afford to pay full rent. I knew Alfredo would not willingly give me any money and I had long since given up hope that his chain of command would help because they had not helped me when he was abusing me. I knew it would not be easy and I did not want to rely on my family for help because I knew where they stood on my marriage. I already knew if I tried to go home again I would probably end up right back with Alfredo, so instead of leaving without a plan, I stayed long enough to gather my resources to ensure that I would not end up back with him. I was leaving and nothing was going to stop me and I promised myself, nothing would make me return.

I recall it was in the fall of the year; it seems like everything bad in my life happened during the fall and that day in 1988 was no exception. I woke up early but I laid in bed pretending to be asleep, waiting for Alfredo to leave for work. When I was sure he was gone, I called my brothers and asked them to come to my house. They helped me pack all of my children's personal belongings along with my own and then took my children to my grandmama's house so they would not be in harm's way. I made up my mind that we had reached the end of the road and I was not willing to live in my abusive marriage anymore. That day was the day I would be leaving by any means necessary and I was not going to run and hide anymore. I was leaving and Alfredo was going to let me go!

I spent part of the day sharpening my knife because I was determined that he was not going to stop me. If I had to fight my way out, then so be it. I also decided I was not going to flee under duress or escape under the cover of darkness, as I had done so many times before. I was going to walk out of the front door with my dignity intact. I wanted Alfredo to know I was no longer afraid of him and his threats would not deter me. I was confronting my abuser face to face because I needed him to understand that I was serious and our marriage was over. I don't know why I thought I could reason with him, but I had been running away for four years only to find myself returning to more abuse time after time! I was not going to *run* again, I was walking away for good and I needed to make him understand that he was not going to stop me.

When he arrived home, Alfredo looked around the room and asked me what was going on. I told him I was waiting to tell him that I was leaving and did not want him to try to stop me or come to my daddy's house. I looked him dead in the eyes when I told him I wanted a divorce because I wanted him to see the resolve in my eyes. Of course, he did not like me looking into his eyes. I think abusers are intimidated by people staring into their eyes, because eyes are the windows to the soul and looking into them can reveal a lot about a person. When I looked into his eyes, I saw exactly what he was hiding behind his bullying ways; self-hate, fear, and insecurity.

Alfredo realized in that moment that I could see how weak he truly was, and he no longer had control over me. He became enraged and, of course, the only thing he had left to intimidate me was his physical strength. When he started yelling and cursing, I knew it was time to make my exit, so I looked for a way out. Alfredo was standing near the front door, so I could not leave that way. I turned and walked down the hallway towards the back door, but he quickly followed me. I walked into the bathroom and tried to close the door, but Alfredo managed to get in and corner me against the bathroom sink.

Whenever he became emotional or angry, Alfredo would talk with his hands, which was a habit I detested because I never knew if he was only talking with his hands or if he was actually going to hit me. Sometimes he would be uttering in Spanish and out of nowhere I would catch a backhand slap, so I was always on high alert when he began waving his hands around.

He was cursing and threatening me and my adrenaline was pumping!! I felt trapped and the hair on the back of my neck stood up. I knew I had to fight and I made up my mind that it was going to be either me or him, so when his hand came up, as to strike, I pulled the knife from my waistband. I slashed Alfredo across the neck with my sharpened knife, sending a gush of blood all over me. I screamed and I remember hearing him scream as well and he immediately ran out of the room clutching onto his neck. I was scared, but I followed him into the other room and when I saw him laid out and the blood gushing out between his fingers, I called 911, and then I called my grandmama. She must have immediately dropped everything and came to my rescue because she arrived within fifteen minutes, a few minutes before the ambulance.

When the paramedics arrived, they wrapped Alfredo's wound while I gathered my things. My grandmama decided that I should voluntarily go to the police station because they were going to issue a warrant for my arrest anyway. When we arrived at the station we spoke to the officer on duty so they could file a report. They "arrested" and fingerprinted me and then released me to go home because my grandmama had a good name and reputation in the county.

If I had been there alone I know for sure they would have arrested me on the spot because I did not paint a typical picture of an abused wife. I was clearly not repentant for what I had done; I was not crying and there were no outward signs of Alfredo's abuse towards me. But what the police did not understand was I did not have any more tears to shed for Alfredo and I was not going to pretend that I was sorry for hurting him because he had hurt me too many times to count.

I was strong when I gave my statement and my resolve was steely! I was tired of that man putting his hands on me and enough was more than enough!

Alfredo ended up spending a couple of days in the hospital and after being released he came out to Holmestown to ask me to come home. Of course, I refused and maybe he knew we had passed the point of no return because he did not push the issue that day. Instead, he went with my grandmama to the police station to try to drop the charges against me. His intention was good, but the state prosecutor decided they would pursue an indictment against me because the cut I made on Alfredo's neck was only centimeters from his jugular vein; I almost killed him.

I was charged with aggravated assault and was told the state intended to prosecute me to the fullest extent of the law. Alfredo apologized profusely and begged me to come back to him, but I refused. There was no turning back from my indictment, so I certainly was not turning back into that abusive marriage!

For the two days Alfredo was in the hospital I had plenty of time to think. I felt like I was having a déjà vu moment. As much as I resented my mama, I mirrored her in so many ways; a marriage during my teenage years, a three times teenage mother, jail... and finally, the worse one of all, I stabbed a man. The only difference is my husband did not die, but they were going to prosecute me anyway, so the realization that I too might be sentenced to prison was unquestionable.

Six years after my mother's conviction for murder, I became a victim of the very same lesson she tried to teach me; trouble is easy to find and sometimes you don't have to go out looking for it. People will bring it to your front door... but in my case, it was in my home all along — brewing underneath the surface, just waiting for the explosion.

Realizing that I had been pushed to the point of almost killing Alfredo made me that much stronger in my conviction to never go back. I stayed with my family for a little while before I ended up going to stay with a friend. Alfredo moved on and began dating someone else and I was happy about that because I was tired of him calling and begging me to take him back. I guess he finally got the message because he stopped bothering me and became another woman's problem. I was more than ready to move on with my life, so I was happy to finally have that burden lifted because I had something more important weighing on me that demanded all of my attention.

At the start of every day, I prayed to God because I knew eventually I would have to face the charges pending against me. I could not afford a good lawyer, so I had a public defender who never had much time to talk and had yet to inquire about what circumstances led me to stab and damn near kill my husband. It did not seem like anyone really cared how we arrived at that violent place, only that we had and as far as they could see, I was to blame. I felt like people dismissed the fact that I was subjected to years of intimidation and abuse from my husband and I grew weary of trying to explain myself because as important as that situation was, it was not first and foremost on my mind.

I was facing yet another mountain that was much bigger and more damaging to my heart and soul than Alfredo's licks had ever been. My children were taken away from me and the separation hurt me deeper than anything I ever experienced. While Alfredo was in the hospital, the Department of Children and Family Services came and took our children because it was determined that our home was not a safe and stable environment for them. I was given weekly visitation while Deville, Ashley, and Freddie were in foster care and it almost killed me not to take my children home, but the fact was I did not have a home to take them to as I was staying with different friends here and there.

Sometimes when it became too much sadness for me to bear, I would drag myself back to Holmestown to stay at my grandmama's house because her presence always made everything better. My life had gotten so out of control that some days I did not know if I was coming or going. With the probability of prison looming, I was not allowed to regain custody of my children, so I could not even plan ahead. I was just living in the moment. Over time I started hanging out with friends and family, drinking and partying, and on more than one occasion I almost landed myself back in jail for an assortment of bad decisions. I was in the streets shoplifting, stealing, and even sold drugs for a little while. I was in and out of relationships and just doing anything I could to take my mind off of my pending trial.

I went to court in April of 1989 with only a public defender in my corner and as I said before, he was not interested in the circumstances that led to our near-fatal encounter. I'm convinced I was just another case on his docket... I was sentenced to five years in prison for the injury I inflicted on my abusive husband to run concurrently with some other charges I had pending. Combined, I was given 16 years for my crimes. I was in disbelief! 16 years was more actual time than they gave my mother for murder! When they read my sentence, my knees buckled beneath me! I could not believe I was going to prison. It seemed like bad luck knew my name personally and did not like me at all!!

I did not begin serving my sentence until a year later in April 1990 because at the time of arraignment, I was pregnant with my fourth child, and, a recent prison death of a young mother and her newborn during childbirth convinced the state that I was a potential liability. I was grateful for the reprieve and used every given moment to try to get in as much living as I could.

I gave birth to my second daughter, Karlissa on December 26, 1989, and signed her over to my mother, on April 24, 1990, which was the day I began serving my 16-year prison sentence at Washington County

State Correctional Facility. At the time I thought it was a blessing that my mama had been released a week prior and would care for my baby until I was finished serving my sentence...But I should have known it would not be that simple.

Prison life was hard, as I was very angry and bitter about the circumstances that landed me there. I missed my children and the rest of my family and I did not think it was fair that Alfredo was out living his life after abusing me consistently over a four-year period, yet when I fought back, I was sent to prison. For the first two years I had difficulty conforming and often got into trouble, but I did not care one way or the other. As far as I was concerned prison was one big, black hole so it did not matter if I was in solitary or the general population, I hated it.

I spent most of my day being angry at the world and the other portion feeling sorry for myself. I felt like I never really had a chance at life. I blamed my upbringing, my mama and daddy, and any and everyone else I could drag into it to keep from looking at myself. True enough, I was dealt a rough hand and many events that occurred in my life were out of my control, but there were also a lot of times I was led by selfishness, lust, and immaturity. Instead of using my circumstances to build a better me, I used it to give credence to the deprived me and to justify my often-poor decisions. For the first two years, I was not willing to take any blame for what happened to me, but eventually someone came into my life who would challenge my way of thinking and help me change my perspective.

I was taken into the warden's office one day after I was involved in yet another confrontation. The warden just looked at me with my clothes hanging off and my hair standing straight up on my head and shook his head. He walked around his desk and looked me dead in the eyes and asked, "Young lady, what is wrong with you?" I didn't know what to say, but I guess he wasn't really expecting an answer. He told me he had kept an eye on me over the last year and saw me heading down a very dangerous path and if I did not get myself together—and he meant quickly, I was going to be past the point of no return.

I was so angry; how dare he try to tell me anything about myself? He didn't know me, but he read me like a book! The warden told me I could look at my incarceration as something bad or I could use it as an opportunity to turn my life around. He said he didn't know what circumstances brought me there, but instead of being angry and fighting all the time, I should be fighting to change my circumstances. Initially, his words hit me hard because I felt like he was blaming me for everything that happened in my life and I wasn't trying to hear that. But once I got out of my feelings I paid close attention to not only what he was saying, but how he was saying it and I realized he was not trying to hurt me; he was there to help.

The warden's words were kind and when I looked into his eyes I did not see pity, disgust, or any of the other looks I saw on a daily basis. I only saw kindness and the God in him, so from that moment on whenever he talked, I listened. I heard everything he said and I truly felt his concern for me. His empathy was genuine and that was something different for me because he did not want anything in return for his kindness except for me to survive and thrive.

I had not listened to anyone's advice or opinions in a long time, but for some reason, the kindness in him spoke to my wounded heart. I felt his compassion for me and it made me want to do better. I wanted to make him proud of me, so I stopped fighting and arguing and worked hard to change my perspective. I used my time to further my education and became a seeker of knowledge. I read every book that I could get my hands on and I began reading the Bible incessantly. I meditated on Philippians 4:13 and learned how to apply what I read to my life and use the knowledge I gained to better myself and change my perspective. I was determined to turn my life around and leave out of prison reformed and renewed.

Book Four

Back to the Honeymoon

I was released from Washington State Correction Facility after serving five years and four months in prison. I was excited to be going home and my heart almost burst out of my chest when I tasted freedom for the first time in five years. I was happy to see my parents, who drove the 2.5 hours to Davisboro, Georgia to pick me up. I had not seen either of them in a long time and as I sat in the backseat of my daddy's car, with my mama riding shotgun like in the old days, I felt like a little girl on an exciting adventure with her parents instead of a young mother just released from prison.

As we drove home I leaned against the window and my mind rested on the one Bible verse that kept me sane while I was in prison. "*I can do all things through him who strengthens me."* I was almost overwhelmed with excitement about the plans I made for my future. I could not wait to embrace my children and find out what was going on in their lives. I wondered how long it would take me to find a job so I could move into my own place. I was excited at the prospect of having all of my children living under one roof and I could not wait to see Grandmama!

Before my release, I thought I had everything figured out! I convinced myself that once I was free, everything would magically transform and I would have the life I imagined while I was incarcerated. Well...let me tell you something, life is no fairy tale, and while I was sitting there being Prison Cinderella, dreaming of a fairy tale ending I had not taken the proper steps to secure the life I told God I was ready to receive.

I walked out of jail thinking I knew my WHY and found my purpose. I decided to blaze a trail in the area that I knew best, domestic violence. It was my goal to help women like me find their way back to who they were before abuse and violence became a part of their lives. It was a lofty goal, but I lived through violence and abuse my entire life, engaged in it and paid the price for it, so in my mind, what more did I need to know? Like I said, I had it all figured out; I was in the starting blocks—READY-TO-GO!

I should have asked myself how I could possibly be ready to help anyone find their way when I had yet to accomplish that goal for myself, but in my excitement to start anew, that particular question never crossed my mind. First of all, I did not realize the depth of the work I had to do to obtain healing for myself. I honestly never put much thought into my own brokenness. I thought being in jail was the majority of my problem and once I was free and able to get a job to take care of my children I would be okay.

In my mind, I believed if I helped others then I would be fulfilling God's will for my life and He would bless me in return. But the Bible says that charity starts at home! I never considered that my past trauma would continue to affect the way I lived and would hinder me from reaching the goals I set for myself because I did not understand the complicated nature of trauma. Coping with deeply rooted suffering is not easy and requires God and some good, old fashioned, God-given talent. That is why our creator made doctors and therapists because *we* must put in the work to assist with our own healing, but we cannot do it alone.

I came out of prison in April 1995 and within a year I found myself occupying another room, compliments of the fine state of Georgia…In other words, I went back to jail. I know you are asking, "How could she possibly wind up back in custody that quickly?" Believe me, I asked myself the same question over and over as I sat for three days in Liberty County Jail. Well, the answer is not an easy one, but I will start by reminding you of the stubborn, single-minded focus I possessed.

Sometimes my determination is a good thing, but other times it is literally a thorn in my flesh that will bother me until I do something about it. Well, when I was released from prison, the first thing I wanted to do was see my children and begin to make up for lost time. They were able to visit me a few times over the years, but it was extremely hard for us to strengthen our bond during the short visitations the state allotted and I missed them so much!

My children were very young when I went to prison, so I missed out on five years of important events in their lives; first days of school, losing teeth, picture days, and school plays for the older ones. Not to mention Karlissa was an infant, so I missed out on hearing her first words, first tooth, walking, potty training, and the list goes on and on! Naturally, when I got out, I made a beeline towards them because I did not want to miss out on another minute of their growth.

I began serving my sentence a month before Deville turned six years old and Ashley and Freddie were about to turn four and three. Karlissa was a newborn when I left so she did not know me, except for the few times she visited me in prison. But my main focus was to get *all* of my children back and have them living under one roof as soon as possible. The day I arrived home, Grandmama immediately stepped aside and relinquished her role as caretaker of Deville and Freddie, who were 10 and seven years old at the time. My mama had my girls and she gave me custody of Ashley without a fight, but that was certainly not the case with Karlissa.

I learned the hard way that she had no intention of giving up custody of my daughter, and for the next seven years, we engaged in an ugly custody battle that further divided our relationship, and also harmed both of our relationships with Karlissa. On my first day out, when we arrived at my parents' house, Mama took me to the side and told me that Ashley could go with me, but she was keeping Karlissa because I signed paperwork giving her custody before I went to jail. She said she was the one raising her and she was the only mother Karlissa knew. I was stunned! I remembered signing paperwork before leaving, but admittedly I didn't read over what it entailed. At the time I was too distraught about going to prison to think about what I was signing.

Finding out that I had signed away full custody devastated me. I could not believe I was so careless! But most of all, I could not believe my own mama would keep me from my child. She told me I had three other children to tend to and I did not know Karlissa. What was worse, Karlissa did not know me either and it was entirely my fault. I don't know why I expected anything different, but I did and when she denied me the right to my daughter, I began to see that getting my life back was not going to be as easy as I thought and the wealth of damage I would have to repair overwhelmed me.

As time went on, I had to admit that my incarceration caused more harm than my conscience wanted me to believe. It tore my little family apart in the same way as my mama's had done to our family 13 years prior. Immediately after I began serving my sentence, Alfredo took Ashley and Freddie to live with him, leaving Deville with my grandmama. Though he doesn't talk about it, I know Alfredo's rejection hurt my son deeply. He was the only father Deville knew, as we married when he was seven months old and by Alfredo taking only his biological children, Deville felt abandoned, like Alfredo did not love him. Losing both of us at the same time had to be devastating to a small child and it breaks my heart to think about it even today.

Why he chose to separate our children like that I can only assume, but given Alfredo's instability, even that arrangement did not last long. Multiple relationships and excessive drinking were some of the root problems my ex-husband allowed to cloud his judgment. I believe he tried to make changes in his life, but it was too little, too late. The environment he provided for Ashley and Freddie was not much better than it was when we were married and eventually The Department of Children and Family Services (DCFS) removed our children from his care. My children experienced traumas too numerous to count while I was away and that is my biggest regret. Conversations between us uncovered so much more than I was ready to accept and for a long time, I was in denial because it was easier that way.

Combined with the hardship of finding a job to provide for us and the weight of the guilt I carried about my children, I was dragging around a lot of baggage. Doors were repeatedly slammed in my face and I felt like time was running out, even though I had just been released from prison. Everything was urgent! I had to immediately get my children, secure a job, find a place to live, and get in a relationship... RIGHT THEN AND THERE! I thought if I could accomplish those things quickly, it would somehow absolve me of the bad things that happened to my children in my absence.

Instead of taking my time, I rushed into everything with little to no preparation, so you can only imagine how many times I had to start over. It was at one of those starting over periods that I was led by God to go see Mr. Mobley, a kind man who owned a convenience store I frequented. I was near tears when I walked into the store and asked to speak to him. I had a lot weighing on my mind because the more I found out about the things my children endured while I was in prison, the stronger I desired the stability that can only be achieved by independence.

More than anything I wanted a place for us to live apart from my family. My children had endured too many incidents of being taken away from loved ones and I did not want them to experience that type of separation again! I wanted them to feel safe and secure with me. While I was incarcerated DCFS was very diligent in keeping tabs on my children and any suspected incidents of neglect or abuse resorted in their removal from my family members' homes. Ashley told me how she was snatched away from my grandmama's house, crying and screaming while she held on to the door jamb for dear life, only to be sent to yet another foster home. I did not want that to happen again. I needed a place to stay right away.

Finding out about the many foster homes and upheaval they lived in and emotional scenes like Ashley described gave me an urgency to find a home so we could experience some stability together. I did not have the financial means to make it happen, so I went to see Mr. Mobley because he had rental properties and my bank account was empty. I needed someone to give me a chance and by the Grace of God, the Mobleys did just that. I told his wife, OkCha I would repay any generosity they could extend to me at tax time. It was only God who led them to provide my family with a fully furnished trailer, complete with a television set for my children. It may not seem like a lot, but for me, it was everything I needed at that moment and I thank God for the Mobley family!

I finally had a place where all of my children could live together and I was excited, but my mama still had a firm grip on Karlissa, so my little family was still incomplete. She was allowed to visit with us from time to time for short periods and it was always emotional when she had to leave. Karlissa enjoyed staying with her siblings, but I do not think she fully understood that I was her mother because my mama had been raising her for five years. She only knew that she loved coming to spend time with us and she wanted it to be permanent. I had several confrontations with my mama about my daughter coming to live with me, to no avail. The only thing our arguments did was upset my children and drive a huge wedge between us.

Over time, I got tired of the back and forth discussions and the pointless arguments, so I decided I was going to take Karlissa from my mama. I was tired of her telling me the child I carried and birthed could not come and stay with me and her siblings, so I made a spur of the moment decision that earned me that room on Airport Road that I told you about earlier.

I went to Karlissa's school to pick her up and the principal called my mama to verify that I had permission to sign her out because my name was not on the list. In the meantime, the secretary called my daughter out of class and she was standing in front of me with a confused look on her face. I still remember the scared look in Karlissa's eyes as we walked towards the front door with the Principal calling for me to stop.

I did not think anyone had a right to question me about my own child, so I kept walking like I did not hear her asking me to stop—that is until my mama walked in the front door, and she was mad as hell! Before it was all over, I was headed back to jail and Karlissa went home with Mama. It was a bad scene. I admit things got way out of hand with me and Mama literally playing tug of war with my innocent child. I know I was wrong for going to the school, but I let my anger and pride cloud my decision making, yet again. Karlissa should not have endured that type of behavior coming from either of us, but pride is a terrible drug.

While I sat in Liberty County Jail for three days I was nurtured by a very kind-hearted jailer. She talked me through the situation and pointed out my mistakes so that I would not repeat them. She provided information on how I could secure my release so I could go home to my children and she told me to seek counsel on my custody situation. I wish I could remember her name, but it has long since faded from memory. While her name escapes me, her kindness is ever-present and I am grateful I had someone on the inside working on my behalf because there were definitely forces on the outside working against me.

While I was locked up, my mama and sister went to my place and removed every bit of my personal property; they took furniture, clothing, and household goods and pawned what they could. Evidently, they believed I would be gone for a long time and had the right to take my things. I was devastated, angry, and ready to fight because some of the things they sold belonged to Mr. Mobley, and their theft put me further in his debt and set me back, yet again.

We were able to resolve the issue without anyone going to jail, but of course, there was a recovery period when I had to fight extra hard to get back on my feet. It seems like I was always going through something and trying to recover. Over the next few years, I continued to live with my children hand to mouth. We struggled financially and moved around quite a bit to avoid eviction. Mama and I continued to argue over my daughter's custody, but as she got older, Karlissa pressured Mama to allow her to live with us. For her

7th birthday, I gave her a party that I am sure made a huge impact on her decision. Mama had converted religions when she was in prison and was a practicing Jehovah's Witness, so she did not celebrate holidays or birthdays. The party I gave Karlissa was her first, so of course, she wanted to stay with us after that. She pressured Mama to allow her to move in permanently with us, and eventually she relented.

Karlissa came to stay with us and I was ecstatic to have all of my children with me. I was so relieved to have her home I didn't think about the fact that I was already struggling; I just wanted my child from my mama — point blank period! However, I wasn't financially stable or mature enough to provide the type of home my children truly deserved. I was working a minimum wage job and barely making ends meet, so I could not afford to properly care for them; sometimes we went without the bare necessities. On top of the financial difficulties, everyone was experiencing adjustment issues that made the transition a little bit bumpy.

Karlissa had to learn to live with and share with three siblings, while also getting to know me as her mother. Mama had to adjust to not having Karlissa with her and she really missed her presence, so she was angry with Karlissa and me. I was more concerned with trying to get to know my child and bonding with her, but that was very difficult because she was used to living a certain way and I could not provide for her in the same manner.

As crazy as it sounds, sometimes I felt like she was judging me and comparing me to Mama. I do not know if it was my guilt or anger that kept us from bonding as we should have, but Karlissa eventually went back to stay with Mama for a while. When I think about it now, I can clearly see I was flying by the seat of my pants. I was focused more on what I wanted than what I could feasibly accomplish. I had no plans in place whatsoever, and failure to plan truly does mean you are planning to fail, and I did, over and over again.

For years I dragged my children around from pillar to post; we moved from house to house and even to different states – chasing opportunities. Well, since I am being transparent, I was chasing more men than opportunities, or perhaps to me, they were one and the same. I dated different men and entertained them at my house; I was always searching for that one who would love and provide for us the way my daddy did when I was younger. I wanted a man who could provide like Alfredo minus the violence and abuse. I desperately wanted to be in a healthy relationship for me and my children, especially my oldest son. I wanted Deville to experience a father's love and the security of knowing that someone truly cared about him.

I never forgot the security I felt when I was a little girl; my daddy always made sure we had more than enough, but after my mama went to prison all I knew was instability. I desperately longed for a lifestyle where I did not have to worry about providing for my children or paying my household bills. I wanted to live without worrying whether or not I had enough food in the house or waiting for the government to send me money to keep my utilities turned on. I hated living from paycheck to paycheck like I did most of my adult life.

I honestly thought the easiest way I could achieve security was through partnership or marriage, so I dated a lot of men in search of a husband who could give me what I lacked. Love took a back seat to security because I thought if I could find a man of means who could provide stability without abuse, then that is all the love I needed. The rest really did not matter because I always felt if there were things I did not like, then I could change him. Notice I said *change him*; not me. With me, it was always about fixing others, but I have since realized that we are only responsible for ourselves. We cannot change people or the way they respond to us. We can only change ourselves and to do that requires a whole lot of growth, self-reflection, truth, and God.

I married my second husband, Samuel Hogan in 1999; two years after giving birth to our son, Antonio (TJ), who is my youngest child. That marriage did not last long, but Samuel did something that none of the other men in my past did; he showed genuine love and concern for my children. From our short marriage, Samuel and Deville formed a lifelong bond and for that, I will always be grateful. I don't know if Samuel is aware, but Deville holds him in high regard because he was always there for him. He knows Samuel cares about him and that is priceless. Even though our marriage ended, I know Samuel genuinely loved us; I just didn't love myself or know how to love in return and that gave way to a lot of other issues that led to divorce.

Truthfully, I don't think anyone could have filled that hole in my heart, but I didn't know it then. I kept telling myself all I needed was someone to take care of me and my children and if he was financially stable, I was willing to try to make it work. But how can damaged people exist in whole relationships? It just doesn't make sense, but back then I was not trying to make sense, I was trying to make ends meet. And as soon as my second marriage ended, I reverted to my old ways. I had a deprived mindset and continued to make poor choices based on my preconceived notions of what I needed to make me happy and content.

Somewhere along the way, I forgot all about the plans I made in prison. I was so focused on trying to provide a stable home that I did not give my children the time and attention they needed and deserved. All the changes and upheaval my children went through during their formative years drove a wedge between us for many years. I can admit that at certain periods of my life I focused on myself more than I focused on anything or anyone else and it was during those times that I crossed over that thin line that separates self-preservation from plain old selfish behavior that I talked about earlier.

Sometimes I did not realize I was alienating my children, but when my daughter Ashley was around ten years old she let me know how she felt about my selfish behavior. I was in my bedroom with a male friend when I heard a loud bang against the door that scared the life out of me. When I went to see what the commotion was, the only thing I saw was Ashley sitting on the couch with one shoe on and her arms folded in defiance. Her other shoe was sitting outside my bedroom door; it was what made the loud bang when Ashley threw it and hit my door. She told me that she threw the shoe because she was tired of me being in the bedroom with men! She told me I always said I wanted to spend time with them, but I was spending more time with men than my children. Ooh, that stung, but it was what I needed to hear to get myself all the way together and I did for a little while.

I guess I never really thought about how it made my children feel when I would take men into my bedroom. I was alienating them the whole time and I had no idea they were even paying attention. I told myself I was trying to find a husband and father for them, but it was *my* attention they wanted and needed, not a man's. But they needed a better version of me and the opportunity for that to happen came from an unlikely source.

I was at home one afternoon in September of 1999 when I heard a knock at the door. When I answered, it was Shonda Mickel, a young lady I knew from high school. I was surprised to see her because we were not really friends and she had never visited my home before. She told me she knew I was surprised, but she came to see me because she wanted to talk about a job opportunity. Shonda told me she was opening up a tax business in December and since she knew I was a go-getter, she wanted me to come and work for her. I was definitely surprised someone thought enough of me to seek me out when it seemed like everyone else shunned me.

Shonda said she would teach me everything I needed to know about preparing taxes and I admit, I was skeptical at first, but I listened to what she was saying. It wasn't until she stated that she knew I spent time in prison and she had also served time that I understood she was sent by God. Shonda knew how hard it was to find a job because she had experienced the same rejection when she got out and that is why she decided to work for herself! When she left, I just sat there and cried; I marveled at how God continued to provide for me, even when I was disobedient. Only another person who shared the same experiences could know how desperate I felt when doors continuously closed in my face, so God sent me just what I needed! Having so many opportunities snatched out of my hands because I was a felon had become commonplace and I was once again feeling trapped inside of my life when God sent a way out.

I began working for Shonda in December, as planned and continued for several years thereafter. True to her word, she taught me everything I needed to become an in-demand tax professional and when I was ready to venture out, she supported my decision.

I can never thank her enough because she gave me an invaluable tool that has sustained me and my family for years. Working for Shonda and learning those valuable job skills gave me a sense of pride that no one can ever take away. Having tax knowledge assured me that I would always be able to work and provide for my family and it did wonders for my self-esteem.

Independence is a feeling that I really cannot explain except to say it made me feel confident; I started evolving. Conversations were different, priorities shifted and I required better treatment from people. Of course, some folks did not understand the changes in me and thought I was being uppity when in reality I was growing into a better version of myself. Honestly, sometimes people don't like to see us grow because it makes them uncomfortable, but that is their problem, not ours. We can't sit around in a little box because it helps others feel better about the box they are living in. For me, there were too many good things happening on the other side of dependence and I am happy that Shonda Mikel offered me an opportunity to feel independence for myself!

Many good things transpired during that period in my life for which I am eternally grateful. When Karlissa was 12, I discovered the custody papers I signed when I went to prison were actually only temporary guardianship. The agreement was dissolved on the day I went into the courthouse to inquire, and Karlissa came to stay with us permanently. Settling the custody issue was like a weight lifting off my shoulders, but I was angry at myself for not checking sooner and beyond angry at my mama for deceiving me for all of those years. But I digress; God's timing is perfect. He knows when we are ready to walk into our destiny and we have to trust His timing in our lives. He evidently knew I was not ready.

Another surprisingly good development occurred when I reached out to my ex-husband, Alfredo for some help with our son. Freddie was struggling through some serious behavior issues, so we came together to co-parent. Believe it or not, within a few short weeks, we reconciled and eventually remarried for several years. God is truly able to do exceedingly and abundantly more than we can ever imagine because He mended our broken relationship and brought us together as if none of the pain occurred in our past. Can you imagine? We fought like animals and I went to prison for almost killing Alfredo, but God saw enough in both of us to hit the reset button and offer us a time to heal those old wounds!

First of all, the changes in Alfredo were astounding; he was calm, kind, and sober—everything I wished he was in the early days. We forged a union that was restorative, albeit temporary, but it gave me a sense of peace about the life I was cultivating for TJ and Karlissa. For the first time, I was able to raise my children and live in an environment that was both calm and stable, which is something I always prayed for. From the time I gave birth to TJ, I was determined to be a better mother and provider; his safety and well-being was a top priority.

His older siblings had experienced so much suffering in their young lives they wanted TJ to have what they did not have and they were not afraid to verbalize their desire to see him treated well. At times I felt like there was some envy between them because TJ definitely benefitted from a better version of me and a calmer home life. I was unable to give my older children any stability, or a father who loved and prioritized them and it was not fair to them at all, but they loved TJ, and the love they have for him outweighs all other emotions.

When Alfredo and I got back together it was because I needed him to step up and help me with our son. Freddie was extremely rebellious and I was at my wit's end because I clearly saw him heading in the wrong direction. I wanted to steer Freddie onto the right path because I had experienced the consequences of unchecked rebellion. Like my own mother, I could see my son's behavior and actions were leading him down the same destructive path I had traveled.

Freddie was very angry and I did not blame him for feeling that way; I just wanted him to see that his anger was going to harm him more than it would anyone else. Like his other siblings, Freddie experienced a lot of trauma; some I probably will never know about, but he has a fierce love for his siblings and it has never wavered. I remember the day I overheard him talking to his father about TJ. He told Alfredo TJ was his little brother and he loved him very much and all he was asking of him was that he be a better

father to TJ than he was to him. He was very emotional and I was openly crying by the time I heard him
say "At least give him what you did not give to me!"
His words simultaneously broke my heart and filled
it with pride for my man-child.

I do not doubt that Freddie's words spoke to his
father's heart, because it seemed like Alfredo worked
extra hard to make sure he presented himself as a
good role model and provider. There was no unpro-
voked violence and unrest in our home; Alfredo told
me he buried that part of himself. He was ashamed
and disgusted by his past actions and as a result, he
stayed away from activities that reminded him of that
violent persona. That included drinking and partying;
he did not indulge in any destructive social activities.

We relocated to Atlanta and then to Florida where
our marriage eventually ended. I loved that we were
living a peaceful and prosperous life, but it seemed
as if all the life had left my husband. I understood
his desire to resist any activities that might alter his
self-control, but outside of work, Alfredo did not
want to go anywhere or do anything that required
him to leave the house. He went into a shell and I felt

trapped inside of that shell with him. I often had to take the children out or go to social events solo because he refused to go. I keenly remember a time when he would not even participate in a family Thanksgiving dinner. I become increasingly frustrated with Alfredo's new way of surviving because it took all of the fun out of life. I became more vocal about my dissatisfactions and soon my frustration turned to aggression and I knew it was time to part ways.

When we reconciled, Alfredo and I made a promise that we would always be honest with each other and we would never result to violence or abuse. When my behavior towards him became hostile and bordered on abuse, I told Alfredo I wanted a divorce because I did not want my behavior to lead us back down that tumultuous path. He understood and did not argue or contest my wishes; he simply agreed and we ended our marriage.

By that time my two oldest children were making their way in the world. Deville was working and taking care of himself and Ashley was attending college in Atlanta. When we left Hinesville a few years earlier Ashley was a senior in high school and did not want to move with us as it could have possibly affected her grades and graduation. She wanted to finish her senior year at Bradwell Institute, so she moved in with her godmother and graduated with her class in 2005, before heading to Atlanta. As much as I missed her I knew she had to make her own way and I was proud of her for taking a stand, even if it was against me.

Book Five

The Calm

After my second marriage to Alfredo ended, my youngest children and I stayed in Florida where we settled into a peaceful, quiet lifestyle. Things were not perfect but it was far from the life we had back in Georgia. It was there I met Araceli Diaz, who became my best friend and business partner. We met at a football game; her son Nahdeem and my son, TJ, were on the same team and for a couple of years we would casually chat at the games. When we began to bond, I shared some of my testimony with Araceli and she encouraged me to share my story with as many people as I could. She thought it was inspirational and would help a lot of young women who found themselves in abusive relationships and I wholeheartedly agreed. Araceli was just as passionate about the subject as I; she would often tell me "Vicki, they need to know there is a light at the end of the tunnel," and she was right. Our friendship set the stage for my next chapter and a lifetime revelation.

As time went on our bond grew tighter and we became inseparable. We shared a lot of intimate conversations and became each other's confidant and sounding boards, but I never imagined the most painful part of my past was something we also shared until the day she revealed the reason she was so passionate about domestic abuse. We were riding in the car one afternoon and I was telling Araceli about some of the petty domestic incidents I endured with Alfredo because some were truly laughable now that I no longer had to deal with them. I was sitting in the passenger seat chatting away when I noticed that Araceli had not commented or laughed at any of my silly comments for a while. When I looked over at her she was driving as if she was in a trance; her thoughts were miles away. I asked her what was wrong and she glanced at me with tears in her eyes and then she looked away.

Araceli pulled over to the side of the road and told me she knew so much about domestic abuse because she was a survivor. When she was younger, she was in a terribly violent relationship that reached a breaking point at one of the most critical times in her life. Araceli was pregnant with her youngest son when a particularly bad fight almost resulted in a miscarriage. She confided that she never told anyone, but it was my willingness to share my experiences that made her comfortable enough to talk about it. I was stunned because Araceli *did not seem* like a person who would be in an abusive relationship, but I had to remind myself that violence and abuse can happen to anyone, even someone as strong as Araceli...and me.

God has a way of placing the right people in our lives to fulfill His will and I believe our meeting and and the subsequent relationship was ordained. That day in the car we started talking about forming an organization to help other victims like us. I confided in Araceli that it was my dream before I was released from prison, but I allowed life to get in the way of my purpose. I believe our coming together was pre-destined because our gifts complemented each other so well. Where I was weak, Araceli was strong and vice versa. Her business acumen was top notch and I am confident and have the gift of gab, so together we could move mountains and we planned to speak out and give a voice to victims of domestic abuse.

For a couple of years, we researched and laid the foundation for our organization that we named, *My Journey~Stop Domestic Abuse*. We wanted to build a business that would provide victims with resources and funding to help them safely separate from their abusers. We examined different types of organizational structures and began putting everything into place to obtain our 501(c) 3 status. We tried to secure grants to provide funding for others, but I never thought about getting help for myself because I had yet to face my own demons or even acknowledge that I had them.

My children were building their own lives; my girls were living together in Atlanta and Freddie and Deville were working and laying foundations for their own families, yet I was still unsettled. I fell into this dysfunctional pattern of starting great projects, but becoming discouraged, or frustrated when met with any small amount of difficulty. And too there was the always present distraction of men who were neither ordained by God, nor even close to being the man whose job was to cover and protect me.

I was in Florida working on establishing my business, but still operating my personal life in the same destructive manner. I knew what I wanted to do professionally, but personally, I was still trying to build a mate and continued to uproot my life for men who I thought could provide security. I became reacquainted with a man from my hometown and after developing a long-distance relationship, I chose to move back to Georgia and interrupt everything I was working hard to establish with My Journey — not to mention, it was TJ's senior year in high school and relocating was the last thing he wanted to do. I'll insert the thin line right here... It hurts, but it's the truth.

I moved back to Liberty County and tried to continue building My Journey. My goal was to become a Court Appointed Special Advocate (CASA) to support women like me who found themselves in abusive relationships, but it was not meant to be. Even though I knew my reason for serving five years in prison was a direct result of my abusive marriage, the fact remained convicted felons are not allowed to be Court Appointed Special Advocates. Everyone at the local organization was aware of the impact my story could have on survivors, but legally they could not make an exception for me and that was devastating.

However, because I applied and often shared my story, people began to recognize my name. I was asked to speak at events and became highly respected as a motivational speaker in my area, but legally I was not allowed to advocate for victims. It felt good to tell my story to crowds, but I truly wanted the right to go speak directly to victims amid their crisis. I wanted to be there directly after violent episodes, in hospitals as they healed from injuries, after being released from the hospital and felt like they had nowhere to go or no one to help, I wanted to be there! It was my goal to offer assistance when they were contemplating leaving those abusive relationships, and when they had escaped to safe shelters. It was during those times that I needed the most assistance — when a good, strong mentor would have been most impactful in the fight against my addiction to abuse. THAT was my focus and when it did not come to fruition, I was disappointed beyond belief.

I have been a victim of violence and abuse of various types, my entire life. I have been hit, punched, kicked, slapped, spit on, and called all types of names. I have been raped, exploited, accused of all types of heinous acts, abandoned, and left to fend for myself and IMPRISONED!!! Yet, I was not good enough to sit and share my knowledge and resources with people just like me. I understood the legality of it; that it was a part of the bylaws, but what I did not and still do not understand is why that aspect is included in the criteria when the very nature of what we strive to achieve involves crime, the judicial system, rehabilitation, and redemption. What better resource can you ask for than one who has walked the walk, talked the talk, and felt the sting of rejection and the pain of bruises?

When I was denied the right to advocate I retreated back to that destructive space where I felt like I was not good enough and honestly, after all the work I put in, my spirit was truly broken. So of course, in true Vicky fashion, the flame for advocacy was extinguished, and might I add, it imploded right along with the marriage I moved home for. Yes, in the midst of birthing My Journey, I married again and I can truly say that marriage was definitely not meant to be; it lasted less than three months. Again, I chose to uproot, relocate, and wed someone based on his ability to provide security, so of course, the marriage failed.

I have come to realize that I never required love in its true essence because I did not know what it was, only that people in my life who said they loved me, made me feel secure, so that is what love looked like to me. Never mind, almost everyone who *said* they loved me did things to hurt me, so love in its true form was foreign to me for a very long time.

The feelings I equated with love came attached to pain, and it is hard to say this, but even the love I shared with my children felt painful back then because I could not provide the security they deserved. I failed my children time and time again because I was too busy searching for me and trying to fill the holes in my heart that I could not provide for their emotional or physical needs. Trying to love them on an empty tank sometimes made me feel useless and insignificant in their lives. God knows I am sorry for all of the sufferings my children endured and I am so thankful He equipped them with the strength and resiliency it took for them to survive and thrive, despite the turmoil I birthed them into.

My children took every brick life threw at them and built a better foundation for their own families. They are definitely better than me and for that I am GRATEFUL! Deville is married to Selena and they are the parents of two of my precious grandchildren. He is a truck driver working overseas and often talks about starting his own business. I have no doubt Deville will succeed because he is resilient and determined. My oldest son is everything he did not have; his children get the best of him and I could not be more proud of the man he has evolved into. Life has not been easy for him but my grandmama Victoria's death marked a turning point in his life. Through every trial Deville faced, Grandmama was there; she never turned her back on him. Her door was always open, but when she passed away Deville knew he had to get himself together, not just to make Grandmama proud, but for himself and his family as well.

Ashley is a wife, mother of three beautiful children, and a two-time college graduate. She works in the hospitality industry but also has a BA degree in English and an AA in Culinary Arts from Le Cordon Bleu. My daughter is smart, funny, and a darn good mother to my grandchildren! After everything she went through as a child, I thank God for restoring all that was lost. He has blessed Ashley with a wonderful husband, Lee and they are raising my three grandchildren, in a healthy, happy environment. I count Ashley as one of my best friends and confidants.

Freddie was the first one to make me a nana and that is an indescribable feeling! My oldest granddaughter is his only child and he is a good father. Freddie works as a landscaper, but like his brother, he desires to work overseas and I'm sure he will get there soon because he can do anything he sets his mind to. Freddie has so much untapped greatness down on the inside and when he discovers it, he is going to be a force! As a woman I know I will never fully understand his struggles as a man, but I hope he knows that I stand with him and I cannot wait to see him come into his purpose!

My youngest daughter Karlssa is the epitome of the word survivor! I know the constant bickering and back and forth custody was hard on her, but by God's Grace she made it through. Karlissa lives in Georgia and works at a credit union while she is pursuing her Human Resources degree. I am happy to say she has recently gotten engaged and I know when the time is right she and her husband will expand their family. I already know she is going to be a great mommy! Our relationship has grown over the years and I am grateful because we had a very rocky start. God knows it could have gone either way, but He saw fit to allow me an opportunity to get to know and love my daughter. I missed out on a lot of Karlissa's life and I know it was not easy on her, but I thank God she gave me a chance...

My youngest son, TJ made his home in Florida; he says that is where home is. We moved around a lot and he had to make sacrifices and adjustments, so I am happy he has a place where he feels safe and grounded. TJ spent a short time in the army, but has found his place in the graphics and gaming industry. He has always been great with technology and one day I expect to see his name on something phenomenal! TJ is married to Taylor and while they don't have any children yet, I look forward to the day they become parents!

I am not perfect, and neither are my children, but for everything we went through I am grateful that we are here, and still have the opportunity to grow together. Our relationships are evolving and flourishing and I will continue to nurture each harvest as they come. Sometimes I wish I could give them the world because they deserve it, but I have no doubts they will reap the desires of their hearts because God has always watched over them and I am thankful for His Grace and Mercy.

Epilogue

Many life-altering things transpired in my life since I moved back home in 2015. I relocated back and forth between Georgia and Florida two times before I finally got tired of running. On my last stay in Florida, I unexpectedly lost my best friend, Araceli to an aneurism and it was a devastating emotional blow. She was my biggest supporter; even when I was at my worst and not the best friend and business partner. Losing her was yet another turning point in my life, emotionally, spiritually, and financially. Because she was the force behind the legal structure of My Journey, it crashed and I lost that very important part of myself. I came home to Georgia broken once again, and that is when I had a Come to Jesus Meeting!!!

It was during that time that I truly accepted Christ in my life and because of that I was able to start rebuilding my relationships. I moved back to Holmestown and spent time with my parents, and siblings and tried to lay down some roots. Along with help from my brother and my former boss, Shonda I was able to start my own legal tax business. With my growth came a desire to go back and close a few chapters in the book of *Vicky.*

Before I left Georgia, I expressed my desire to apply for a pardon from the state for my crime against Alfredo and some other charges I amassed when I was young and foolish. In all of my starting and stopping, that particular goal was placed on the shelf, but after Araceli died I began to see the uncertainty of life and I knew if I wanted a chance at true happiness I had to face myself and all of my demons. As much as I wanted to stay home and make amends with my family, there was too much pain attached to home, so I left, but not before receiving the awakening God led me home to receive.

One day I looked in the mirror and all I saw were excuses and failures; up until that point I allowed my past to dictate my future and I was exhausted. I was tired of running and struggling financially, but most of all I was spiritually drained. I always knew how to pray but I fell into the habit of calling on God when I *thought* I needed Him. I had to get back in my word and stop being an intermittent Christian because the truth is I need Him every hour of every day! His Grace and Mercy sustain me and give me strength and courage to do the work!

I had to face myself! As I stood looking in that mirror, I prayed and cried. Instead of making excuses, I peeled back the layers little by little, and it was hard! I looked into my own eyes like I did Alfredo and faced my fears, doubts, and weaknesses. I confronted *Vicky* and then I acknowledged the parts I played in my broken marriages, broken family ties, and relationships; I am sometimes selfish and stubborn to a fault and I know relationships require work! But when it was all said and done, I reminded myself to show *Vicky* a little bit of Grace because she has been through a lot and nevertheless, she is STRONG, WORTHY, IMPERFECT, AND HEALED, just as God sees her!

I clearly saw Grandmama Victoria's eyes staring back at me that day. I heard her voice telling me "Vicki, don't forget your assignment!" My grandmama transcended this world on February 7, 2009, and I have missed her presence every single day of my life, but on that day in 2017, she was very much alive! Grandmama Victoria was my rock and as I stood in the mirror, I heard her voice reminding me that I was her namesake and as such, I am special. When I was a little girl, she told me I was born with a veil over my face and it was a rare blessing! I did not know what any of it meant at the time, but she always told me when I was going through tough times to remember how rare I was. She said I had inherent strength, and I needed that kind of Godly strength to do His will. Over the years she cautioned me about my gifting, but in my brokenness, I did not understand how I could be chosen to do anything for anyone because I could not even do for myself.

I have learned that God can and often does use the broken to fulfill His will and that is exactly why I was not ashamed when I once again went back and began again!! I started slowly by first increasing my prayer life. Then I began working on being a better version of myself by making amends, telling the truth, and admitting my faults. I started dealing with my trust issues that stemmed from years of abuse through therapy. I applied and received my pardon from the state of Georgia on May 30, 2018, and made plans to relaunch My Journey. On May 24, 2019, I married a wonderful man who shows me every day what it means to really love and cover someone as the Bible commands.

I am nearing year two in my marriage with my husband, Brian and I could not be happier building a life and a farm with him. When I think back to all of those days I spent on my grandfather's farm, and how I loved playing in the dirt and witnessing new growth, I am certain I am living my destiny. Brian definitely did not come in the package I expected, but through my renewed relationship with God, I learned that I had to let go of my expectations to make room for God's will to be done in my life. Sometimes I still have to resist the urge to stick my hands in and try to stir the pot that God has so graciously provided to our little family because I am only human and that fiery, feisty little girl who always wanted to do things her way still takes up a small corner residency in my heart. Y'all, please continue to pray for me (and her)!

In the meantime, I have learned to trust God; I trust that He has given me just what I need and His Grace is sufficient. He is faithful, and has been so good to me! I thank Him for placing people in my life who looked beyond my circumstances and saw that wounded little girl. There were quite a few angels placed along my path to now that guided, inspired, and held me up until I was strong enough to stand on my own, and I desperately want to pay their kindness forward.

I am saying a special prayer of gratitude to my grandmama in heaven, the fatherly warden, the compassionate DCFS social worker, the clerk at the jail who helped me find resources to get free the second time, the kindhearted landlord, the business owner who gave me career skills, my co-author, my business partner, my husband, and my children have all been instrumental in helping me get to know and love Vicky. FATHER GOD, YOU KNOW EACH OF THEIR NAMES AND WHERE TO FIND THEM. I ASK THAT YOU BLESS EACH OF THEM ABUNDANTLY...

One day at a time is my commitment to my never-ending healing. Learning to love someone in all of their faults is not easy, especially when that someone is you and you know all the tea!!! But God is continually working on me. Every now and then I think about my dream of being a CASA and how important it was to me back then...God is showing me every day how to be content with each blessing as they come, no matter how big or small. And I know if and when it is time, He will lead me back to that road.

I'm also learning to swerve, as my forever First Lady, Michelle Obama stated in her book, *Becoming*. There are more routes than one to your intended destination and if God constructs a roadblock, it just might mean He wants you to slow down or take an alternate route. If I had known better I would have understood that He brought me to advocacy, so He made provisions.

In my single-minded focus, I saw their no as NEVER; I viewed it as rejection instead of redirection. In the interim, I can see that God provided all the support I needed. But as usual, I was expecting my impact to be made my way, and when He offered me His portion (a stage to speak), I accepted, but still coveted that title, advocate. Had I trusted God fully back then I have no doubts He would have made that stage a lot bigger, but now I understand; I was not ready, but God's timing is always perfect.

Like I said in the beginning, my life has played out like the five stages of domestic abuse, and I am sure many of you who face the same battles every day. My advice is to **love yourself** and **love your children** so that they know what real love looks like and won't be fooled by wolves in sheep's clothing. **Don't be so quick to give your heart to the first person who speaks to your flesh**. Wait on the one who is willing to grow with you and help you to lay down some of your baggage. **Be diligent and watchful** so that when you see potential risks to your happiness and safety you can avoid it.

Make the hard decisions to walk away from people and situations that hurt and harm your body or your soul. Sometimes you have to let it burn. I would much rather have a broken heart from leaving than one that is broken *and* battered because I stayed. **Trust yourself**; God gave us the gift of discernment, so if it does not feel or look right, don't make excuses and don't try to look at it from all angles! It probably is exactly what you think it is. **Stop fooling yourself** into believing things are going to get better. They won't get better until your abuser decides to get better. In the meantime, you make the best decision for you! **Trust your first judgment** and move on! If someone is hurting you, don't spare their feelings, **TELL SOMEONE!** Our silence is complicity! Don't give abuse room to grow! Speak up because that is the only way to silence abuse.

I know it is not easy and sometimes I believe the progression of time and evil in the world makes it just that much harder for people suffering from abuse. The added element of social media makes bullying and abuse even more common and damaging, not to mention the Pandemic!! I cannot imagine having to quarantine with my abuser, and my heart truly goes out to anyone who is surviving through these times!! But please, don't be afraid or ashamed of anything you have been through, especially not ending a situationship that is causing you harm! LOOK AT ME; I'VE BEEN THROUGH IT ALL AND SEEMS LIKE

I'VE DONE IT ALL...In fact, there is so much more to my story, more trauma, more bad decisions, and yes, more skeletons! But guess what, God still loves me and He has so much more in store for me and I can promise you, He feels the same way about you!!

So this is me, starting over again. I am standing with my arms outstretched waiting and anticipating the overflow. This time I am acting in full obedience and ready to do things differently. God said to share my story and to tell others who are just like me; bruised, battered, rejected, and battle-weary that there is peace and purpose on the other side of pain. We all deserve to live a life that is free of abuse and violence! I am a living witness to God's deliverance but I am just one voice speaking on His behalf. Prayerfully, my voice is strong enough to resonate in even the darkest of places!! Yes, Beautiful, I am talking to you!!!! Don't be afraid to put in the work, because God is able and YOU are deserving!

STATE BOARD OF PARDONS AND PAROLES

PARDON

WHEREAS, Vicky Laverne Gonzalez (aka – Vicky Golden; Vicky Hines; Vicky Hogan), Serial Number EF-258405 was convicted in the court(s) indicated below of the following offense(s) for which he/she received the sentence(s) hereinafter set forth:

OFFENSE	COURT OF CONVICTION	DATE SENTENCE BEGAN	SENTENCE
Theft by Shoplifting (2 cts.), Simple Battery - 1-110987	Chatham Superior	11/09/1987	51 months probation on each count. Terminated - 05/07/1992
Aggravated Assault (ct. 1) - 90-R-5864	Liberty Superior	04/25/1990	5 years to serve, concurrent with sentence previously imposed. Terminated –04/23/1996
Burglary (cts. 1 & 2) - 89-R-5742	Liberty Superior	04/24/1990	6 years to serve followed by 2 years probated on each count (cts. 1 & 2). Terminated –04/23/1996
Sale of Cocaine (ct. 2) - 89-R-5744	Liberty Superior	04/24/1990	3 years to serve followed by 2 years probated, consecutive to 89-R-5742. Terminated –04/23/1996
Burglary (cts. 1 & 2), Forgery (cts. 3-5), Theft by Deception (cts. 6 & 7) - 90-R-5840	Liberty Superior	04/24/1990	5 years to serve (ct. 1), consecutive to 89-R-5742 & 89-R-5744, 5 years to serve (ct. 2), concurrent to count 1, 2 years to serve (ct. 3) consecutive to cts. 1 & 2, 2 years to serve (ct. 4), concurrent to ct. 3, 2 years to serve (ct. 5), concurrent to ct. 3, 12 months to serve (cts. 6 & 7), concurrent to ct. 1. Terminated –04/23/1996
Forgery in the First Degree (cts. 1-4) - 90-R-5987	Liberty Superior	10/30/1990	5 years to serve each count. Terminated - 10/29/1995
Burglary (cts. 1 & 2), Theft by Taking (ct. 3) - 90-R-031	Long Superior	04/24/1990	5 years to serve one each count (cts. 1-3), concurrent to each other and with any other sentences now serving. Terminated –04/23/1995

and,

WHEREAS, an application for a Pardon has been filed by the above named individual; and

WHEREAS, having investigated the facts material to the pardon application, which investigation has established to the satisfaction of the Board that the pardon applicant has been crime free for 22 years, maintained continuous employment, established involvement in civic, religious and or community organizations, made education improvements, is a law-abiding citizen and is fully rehabilitated;

THEREFORE, pursuant to Article IV, Section II, Paragraph II (a), of the Constitution of the State of Georgia, the Board, without implying innocence, hereby unconditionally fully pardons said individual, and it is hereby

ORDERED that all disabilities under Georgia law resulting from the above stated conviction (s) and sentence (s), as well as, any other Georgia conviction (s) and sentence(s) imposed prior thereto, be and each and all are hereby removed; and

ORDERED FURTHER that all civil and political rights, except the right to receive, possess, or transport in commerce a firearm, lost under Georgia law as a result of the above stated conviction(s) and sentence(s), as well as, any other Georgia conviction(s) and sentence(s) imposed prior thereto, be and each and all are hereby restored.

It is directed that copies of this order be furnished to the said applicant and to the Clerk(s) of Court(s) in the County(s) where the above sentence(s) were imposed.

GIVEN UNDER THE HAND AND SEAL of the State Board of Pardons and Paroles, this 30th day of May, 2018.

STATE BOARD OF PARDONS AND PAROLES

Caryl Deems

FOR THE BOARD_____
　　　　　　　　　　Caryl Deems

GET HELP

If you or someone you love needs help,
call the National Domestic Violence Hotline at

1.800.799.SAFE (7233)

TTY 1.800.787.3224

Photos

Vicki working as a gym aid in the Washington State Correctional Institute.

Deville, Ashley, Freddie and TJ in a park in Boston Massachusetts. Circa 2000.

Washington State CI visitation. L-R back row: Aunt Vanessa, Vicki, Cousin Tunesia. 1st row L-R: Freddie, Deville, Karlissa, and Ashley (1994).

Vicki's Surprise 50th Birthday Party in Atlanta Ga. All children minus TJ along with Grandchildren, London and Noah (Deville) and Ernest V and Elliott (Ashley).

Freddie, Ashley and Deville and Vicki at the park for
granddaughter London's birthday party (2018).

Araceli and Vick heading out for a night of fun.
Largo, Fla. (2016).

Brian and Vicki, at home in Quitman, Texas (2020).

Vicki and TJ's selfie (2019).

CPSIA information can be obtained
at www.ICGtesting.com
Printed in the USA
BVHW090416211220
596045BV00005B/12

9 781736 166703